·THE·ORIGINAL·DIET·

·THE·ORIGINAL DIET·

RAW VEGETARIAN GUIDE
AND RECIPE BOOK

KAREN CROSS WHYTE

ILLUSTRATED BY BILL YENNE

TROUBADOR PRESS  SAN FRANCISCO

Library of Congress Cataloging in Publication Data

Whyte, Karen Cross.
    The original diet: raw vegetarian guide and recipes

    Bibliography: p. 97
    Includes index.
    1.   Cookery (Natural foods)   2.   Food, Raw.
3.   Vegetarian cookery.   4.   Diet.   I.´ Title.
TX741.W49   641.5'636   77-4415
ISBN 0-912300-77-9
ISBN 0-912300-76-0 pbk.

Book design by Lorena LaForest Bass

FOR MARY

CONTENTS

❧

FOREWORD

From the beginning, people have always had a diet that was substantially plant based. While a large portion of all ancient diets we know about has included raw foods, this portion has become dangerously small in the diets of people living in urban industrial society.

The dangers of narrow, increasingly refined, almost fiberless eating can be offset by the beneficial effects of increasing raw vegetable foods in every diet.

Focusing on simple, easy-to-digest, delicious and economical raw vegetarian recipes, this book details an exciting, healthy new direction from our pre-historic past.

The author of *The Complete Sprouting Cookbook* and *The Complete Yogurt Cookbook* has a thoroughly researched and fresh point of view for both the committed raw food vegetarian and those who will wish to enhance their eating and health by trying these receipes.

—The Editors

INTRODUCTION

The original diet of raw vegetable food is less expensive, easier to prepare and saves more energy than a conventional cooked diet. But, are raw foods the most natural diet for man? Why is a vegetarian diet best for man?

Since the dawn of creation no animal other than man has cooked. This custom is unique to man, but man's digestive system is not unique. It is still biologically the same as other primates. Raw foods are the most natural for all animals; man is no exception.

The human body is such a marvelous system that an individual can survive, for a while, on almost any kind of food under the most adverse conditions. But, for an individual to live in good health, he should select most of his food from the plant kingdom and eat it raw. Man's ancestors provided him with a system ideally suited to utilize the nutrients of raw fruits, vegetables, nuts and seeds.

It may be difficult to adhere to a raw vegetarian diet today. However, when you are successful in attaining even a part of this goal, the rewards in improved health make the effort worthwhile. If persistent in your efforts, your diet will eventually evolve into one that is best for you. You can once again eat the primarily raw vegetarian diet of our heritage, the original diet.

—*Karen Cross Whyte*

THE DIET EVOLUTION

THE FIRST PRIMATES

We must look to evolution to tell us the origins and development of modern man's diet. By retracing our steps to the very beginnings of the primates, we can discover what foods most likely made up the diet of our progenitors. It is difficult to draw a straight line from the earliest primates to modern man. But, by examining the primates that shared the same general lineage, we are able to learn much of man's dietary heritage.

The first primates are known to us only through a single fossilized tooth, approximately 150 million years old, found at Purgatory Hill, Montana. Its owner was a contemporary of at least six species of dinosaur. The tooth is a spatulate canine, a type common to fruit and leaf eaters and never found among carnivores, so it can be assumed that the first primates were vegetarians.

The early fossil record of the first primates is scanty, but by the Paleocene epoch, 70 million years ago, there are sixty known genera. They evolved from preprimate forms similar to present-day volves, moles, hedge-hogs, and shrews. The preprimates' teeth were suited for eating seeds and insects. The early primates were tree-climbing prosimians who lived in enormous tropical forests. They looked like modern tarsiers, lorises, lemurs, and bushbabies, which eat fruit, seeds, buds, shoots, leaves, grubs and slow-moving insects, and occasionally an egg or baby bird. Probably the best-known species is *Plesiadapis,* a fruit-eater whose projected rodent-like incisors were excellent for hulling fruits such as pomegranates. His molars and premolars were well suited to grind the pomegranate seeds.

1

Over the millennia, gradual changes took place. From the prosimians evolved the transitional forms of the ancestors of modern apes and monkeys. The earliest monkeys were probably frugivorous (fruit eating), and the earliest apes were herbivorous (leaf eating). Modern monkeys and apes, although predominantly vegetarian, occasionally eat bird eggs, fledglings, some meat, and even small quantities of soil containing salt. Many fossils of these early primates have been found in Fayum Basin in Egypt, which 30 million years ago was a lush tropical forest with lazy meandering rivers, a Garden of Eden that was the home of eight species of primates and an abundance of water-loving animals such as crocodiles, rhinos, and miniature elephants. The primates at Fayum were probably utilizing the branch tips for food. Since branches and twigs cannot bear much weight, they were at a disadvantage in gathering the food of the trees. However, this problem could be overcome if the animal hung from the branches above and at the same time stood on the branches below. This type of feeding habit apparently led these primates toward a more erect posture.

During the Miocene epoch, the world's great forests began to shrink. The new, open woodlands on forest fringes and the grassy areas around lakes become the home of *Dryopithecus,* the next well-known genus. The dryopithecines lived in Asia, Africa, and Europe 18 million years ago. Over 500 fossils of this type have been recovered by archaeologists. In 1948 Mary Leakey found in Africa a nearly complete skeleton. The fossil records show there were at least six different species of dryopithecines. The dryopithecines had comparatively small incisors and molars similar to those of modern man. They differed in their projecting canine teeth, which may have been used for defense as well as for tearing open fruit. This tooth arrangement made a rotary grinding and chewing motion impossible, so it is probable that the dryopithecines were frugivorous.

The final primate on the path leading to the family of man is *Ramapithecus.* He is represented by only four fossil fragments, found in India, Turkey, Greece, and Africa. The ramapithecines apparently overlapped in time with the family of man. The northernmost and southernmost part of their range was temperate and would not have supported a principally frugivorous diet. In temperate climates fruits are seasonal, and large apes would have had to turn to other food sources. *Ramapithecus'* teeth show a definite transition toward the human pattern. The canines are small

and do not project, enabling him to chew from side to side rather than limiting him to the up-and-down motion. Based on this evidence and on the form of the grinding molars, it seems that the ramapithecines were becoming ground feeders. Their teeth were ideally suited to eating seeds, grains, and roots.

It is clear that from 150 million years ago until the emergence of the family of man, about 5 million years ago, early primates were overwhelmingly vegetarian. Today, some of the smaller primates are insect eaters, and some species will eat meat if given the opportunity. Their digestive systems are capable of dealing with high protein meat diet for a limited time. However, in general, primates are meat eaters by rare accident. By the time man emerged, his progenitors had provided him with a biological system that was well suited to the utilization of the nutrients of food from the four classic vegetable categories: leaf, fruit, root, and seeds.

AUSTRALOPITHECUS

The australopithecines lived in Africa from approximately 5 million years ago to about 1.5 million years ago. Perhaps no time in our evolutionary history has caused more excitement and controversy among researchers than this period. New materials are constantly being recovered and new theories published about this tool-using species.

Sites such as Omo, Hadar, and Olduvai are internationally famous, as are the researchers who have investigated them. From these and other sites, an astounding number and variety of australopithecine fossils have been found. The fossil records show that there were two kinds of individuals living during this time. It is not clear whether these two types were of different species. Perhaps their differences were no more than the differences between male and female within their own group. The important fact is that both types were evolving along the path that led to early man.

These two types of Australopithecus shared many traits. Their teeth were similar in shape to those of modern man. Fossil remains of the neck and skull show that it was possible for australopithecines to make voluntary sounds. The bones of the pelvis, leg, and foot indicate that they could walk on two legs, and the bones of the hand show that they were able to use their hands as we do.

The two species differed primarily in size. One was small, weighing perhaps 27 kilograms (60 pounds). The other was more robust, weighing up to 64 kilograms (140 pounds), with a more powerful jaw. The overall size of the jaw and the size and location of muscle attachment on the skull reveal that he was able to move the jaw in almost any direction. This suggests that his diet was herbivorous — more specifically, that he fed on small tough morsels like stems, seeds, and corms. The lighter individual's jaw and tooth pattern show that lateral and rotary motion were also possible. The jaw and teeth were smaller, which may account for the less strongly developed masticatory and neck muscles. The small australopithecine diet was probably also basically vegetarian.

Being bipedal, it is possible that at least some of the australopithecines lived as omnivorous scavengers or as hunters and gatherers. The modern Bushmen of the Kalahari and the Australian aborigines consider themselves to be primarily hunters, although they depend on fruit and plants for 60 to 80 percent of their diet. It is a mystery why such strong emphasis has been placed on hunting in the development of man. One researcher, David Pilbeam, has stated:

> The importance of hunting has perhaps been overemphasized in discussion of hominid evolution; undoubtedly, many of the implements used by hominids were meat preparing tools, yet the technology involved in plant collecting and perhaps in its preparation was perhaps equally important. Much of the plant food available in open country required quite a complex preparation — crushing, soaking, and so forth — and this aspect of the hominid's developing technological skills should not be overlooked.

The Leakeys found tools suited for digging, crushing, and pounding vegetable food in great numbers at Olduvai Gorge, as well as the much fewer, but somehow better known, possible meat-preparing tools.

The australopithecines, then, can be conceived of as a variation on a theme. That theme was basically vegetarian and, in some cases, almost certainly herbivorous; it included omnivorous scavenging and possibly hunting. By the end of their era australopithecines could be termed eclectic feeders.

HOMO ERECTUS

The earliest bands of *Homo erectus* emerged during the middle of the Pleistocene epoch (Ice Age) about one and a half million years ago. They are thought to be the descendants of the most advanced australopithecines. *Homo erectus,* generally known by the names Peking Man and Java Man, lived in tropical areas of Africa and in the temperate areas of Asia and Europe. For the first time in archaeological history, man's ancestors were confronted with a hostile environment. Their natural response to the bitter cold of the Ice Age was to use the magical tool, fire, and to develop the skills of hunting.

Homo erectus was about 1.68 meters (5.5 feet) tall. From the neck down he looked much like modern man, but he had no chin and a sloping forehead. The large size of his brain (approximately 1,000 cubic centimeters) and the shape of his neck suggest that slow speech was possible. Modern man can vocally transmit about thirty sounds per second. *Homo erectus* would have communicated more slowly, at about 10 percent of our usual speed. His ability to speak was probably responsible for his great progress in cultural and technological skills.

Fossil finds above Nice, in France, at Terra Amata, give us one of the most complete pictures of these people. For one thing, they built hearths. The remains around these hearths show that *Homo erectus* ate birds, turtles, rabbits, red deer, mountain goat, elephant, boar, rhinoceros, and wild ox, and also seafood such as fish, oysters, limpets, and mussels. Specimens of fossilized human excrement were found to contain fossil pollen of yellow broom, an excellent source of protein, vitamins, and minerals. In other locations, *Homo erectus* ate an abundance of hackberry seeds. In certain areas during the winter vegetation was no doubt scarce, but *Homo erectus* was clearly not exclusively carnivorous.

The biggest factor in *Homo erectus'* shift from a basically vegetarian diet to an increasingly omnivorous one seems to be connected with his living in a temperate climate. Fruits and most vegetation were not available during the winter months. Since game was available, the alternative was to turn to hunting in an effort to supplement the unstable vegetable diet.

Man and a few monkeys and apes that have been tested are unable to synthesize vitamin C, an ability that almost all other animals have. The gene that controls the final step required to manufacture this vital substance is lacking. It is possible that *Homo erectus* also lacked this ability, and, without a constant supply of fresh vegetation, that he, like modern man, could get scurvy and die. Probably *Homo erectus* gathered fresh, young plants from beneath the snow as deer survive during the winter by scraping away the snow with their hoofs to reach the green vegetation beneath.

The mastery of fire has been attributed to *Homo erectus.* There has been some speculation that *Homo erectus* learned how to control fire when sparks from making stone tools ignited fur or brush. However, the first flint stone has a date associated with modern man. Fire kept him warm and protected him from predators. Charred bones have been found dating back 500,000 years, and the earliest hearth was tentatively assigned to 750,000 years ago.

It is not known exactly when or why man first cooked his food. Perhaps he cooked to provide hot food during the cold winters, or to soften fibrous meat and to introduce new flavors, or perhaps simply to preserve meat.

British anthropologist Edmund Leach feels that there may have been another reason. He said:

> It isn't a biological necessity that you should cook your food, it is a custom, a symbolic act, a piece of magic which transforms the substance and removes the contamination of 'otherness'. Raw food is dirty and dangerous: cooked food is clean and safe . . . man somehow saw himself as 'other' than nature. The cooking of food is both an assertion of this otherness and a means of getting rid of anxiety which otherness generates.

It is possible that *Homo erectus* ate meat and cooked as a response to the problems of food during the cold months of a temperate climate and to remove himself from nature. Today we have the technology to make another response. Modern transportation systems are so advanced that there are few places in the world where fresh vegetables are not available the year round. We are beginning to accept ourselves as a part of nature. We can again eat a raw vegetable diet.

HOMO SAPIENS

"What is man that Thou art mindful of him?" Many theories have been advanced by man in his search for himself and his origins. Is man his ability to make and use tools? Is he his large brain and upright walk? Is he a primate with the ability to speak and laugh? He is perhaps all of these things in combination, but the sum may be more than merely the parts added together.

Homo sapiens first emerged about 450,000 years ago, in the middle of the last Ice Age. This early man is known as Neandertal man; he lived in Europe, Asia, and the Middle East until about 40,000 years ago. He is often the prototype of a cave-man cartoon character, but this notion is not correct. It was during this period that man's brain grew to modern size (1,400 cubic centimeters). Although rather burly and heavy-set, by the end of this period Neandertal man was fully modern except that he lacked a chin.

One of the most important changes in the way Neandertal man looked is that the size of his jaw reduced to become modern in size. Was his small jaw related to the omnivorous, mostly cooked, softer diet? Maybe it was. At least one researcher, however, feels that jaw size may have reduced as more and better tools were developed and replaced the teeth as cutting instruments. Teeth are still used by Eskimo groups to cut meat and soften leather by chewing. In the beginning Neandertal man had only a few tools, but as he progressed he developed over sixty different types of tools, including tools that were useful only to make other tools.

Neandertal man hunted in groups, generally choosing the larger herd animals as game because of their high food yield. It has been estimated that a band of twenty-three persons required 225 kilograms (500 pounds) of meat a week to maintain adequate health, approximately 1.4 kilograms (3 pounds) of meat per person per day, or at least 225 grams of protein. Nutritionists have discovered that when the daily protein intake is around 100 grams, there is a tendency for calcium to be excreted from the body. To prevent a calcium deficiency, Neandertal man would have had to eat enough leafy vegetables to bring his total calcium intake to 3,000 to 3,360 milligrams per day. Leafy greens are high in calcium but they were scarce during his time and it would take the equivalent of 1.8 kilograms (4 pounds) of collards to provide 3,000 milligrams of calcium. Insufficient calcium causes bone to malform and become brittle and fragile. Several Neandertal skeletons have been found with deformities of the vertebrae and jaw, suggesting that Neandertal man may have suffered from deficiencies in calcium. In addition, he may have suffered from insufficient vitamin C, which is found in fruits and vegetables. During the darker winter months he may not have received enough sunshine for his skin to manufacture vitamin D. Vitamin deficiencies lower man's resistance to diseases, and the lack of the nutrients found in fresh plant food may have contributed to a short life span.

Neandertal appears to have been a sensitive, loving human being. There is evidence that he cared for the disabled and buried his dead with flowers. One male skeleton was taken from Shanidar Cave in Iraq. The buried man was estimated to be forty years old when he died. In addition to arthritis and blindness of the left eye, his arm and shoulder were deformed from birth and had never grown. His very worn teeth suggest that he used them to compensate for his arm. His skull shows a concussion that healed before his death. Such an individual would be of little practical use to his band, yet he was obviously cared for and lived to a relatively old age.

Neandertal man stored surplus food in what must have been the world's first root cellars. To make root cellars, he selected a cave or made a hole in the ground and lined it with flat rocks. Food was then placed in the cellar and, to protect it from scavengers, it was covered with a heavy layer of rocks that provided a well-insulated storage chamber.

Despite Neandertal man's hard life, it seems clear that his progress was accelerating. By 40,000 years ago modern *Homo sapiens* was an accomplished craftsman who worked with ivory, bone, wood, leather, and pottery. From these materials he created beauty in his tools, clothing, and shelter. He left paintings in caves and on rocks of such beauty and sophistication that when discovered they were at first thought to have been painted by contemporary artists.

Homo sapiens spread out over the world, adapting his life-style to each part of the earth and to varying climates, in the way he dressed, hunted, constructed his dwellings, and in the food he gathered. He was fully omnivorous; he ate every sort of food. When an area was exhausted of game or vegetation, he moved on to new food supplies or followed game into new areas. In warm regions, he was a food gatherer and harvester. Where there were grasslands, he harvested and milled seeds and possibly made unleavened bread by baking the dough on hot stones. He may even have made beer from wild grains. He moved into Siberia where meat was plentiful and vegetables were scarce. He was persistent and confident regardless of the climate. He was a success.

One of the best ways to understand what man was like in this distant time, before the advent of agriculture, is to look at a group of hunters and gatherers who survived into modern times. The Kung Bushmen of the Kalahari Desert in Africa are good examples of modern-day hunter-gatherers, since hunting provides 30 to 40 percent of their diet. It is not unreasonable to postulate a similar percentage for prehistoric hunters.

Kung Bushmen live in an arid environment, yet they have year-round reliable food sources. The time needed to gather their food is surprisingly small. Only adults provide food; youngsters and unmarried people are not required to participate in these activities. To provide enough food for all, adults spend on an average of 12 to 19 hours a week hunting and gathering. The men hunt medium and large game and gather a few plants. The women gather only plant food, but they provide two or three times as much food, by weight, as men. Hunting is not always successful; gathering is. The food can usually be found within a day's walk from the camp. The Kung Bushmen eat fifty-nine species of fruit, berries, and melons, and thirty species of roots and bulbs. The major protein plant food is the mongongo nut (magetti), which is so plentiful that thousands of pounds are left unharvested. The mongongo nut contains 56 grams of protein per 210 grams (7½ ounces), the equivalent of 390 grams (14 ounces) of lean beef. Theoretically the Bushmen could survive on vegetable food alone and still have an enviable amount of leisure time.

During the period between 450,000 and 10,000 years ago, man became more and more flexible in his ability not only to survive, but also to succeed with a sense of accomplishment and fulfillment. The stage was thus set for man to begin to control his food resources — the agricultural revolution began.

THE AGRICULTURAL REVOLUTION

Many cultural myths and legends have grown up around the origins and development of agriculture. Some of these myths suggest that the knowledge came from a benevolent deity, one of them Ceres, the Roman goddess of grain and agriculture. While the belief in mythical deities has generally been supplanted by scientific knowledge, some cultures still seek supernatural aid to produce abundant crops. In any case, how and why agriculture began are questions that have intrigued man for centuries. *When* is easier to determine than *how.* Charred grains of wheat have been unearthed and carbon-dated to about 10,000 years ago. These grains were not of the wild variety, so the age of farming is at least equal to this date. One of the first places where agriculture began was in the Fertile Crescent, a water- and soil-rich area in the Near East arching from the western coast of the Mediterranean eastward around the Syrian desert to Iraq. Soil and climatic conditions in this area were not favorable to food gathering, so cultivation was attempted.

Changing climatic conditions may have forced wandering tribes to turn to agriculture. The pressure of famine may have settled the nomads, forcing them into farming and dependency on grains for most of their protein. To support an increasing population, perhaps new ways had to be found to encourage nature to produce more food on the same amount of land — irrigation, for example. The ancient free-roaming way of life was abandoned forever in favor of the stocked larder and the full stomach.

Basic knowledge of agriculture was probably in existence long before farming actually began. Living as he did, close to the earth, man must have gained a vast amount of knowledge about plants and animals. Primitive peoples are not casual observers of nature, since their lives depend on knowing the essence of their food supplies. Nomadic tribes knew where wild grains grew and returned year after year to harvest them. They knew when fruits and nuts were in season. Following herds of wild animals, they would have observed and no doubt studied their habits. They would have observed how wilted plants revived after a summer rain. While gathering wild wheat, women may have watched the wind separate wheat seed from the chaff and scatter the seed through the air. Wheat and oats are naturally constructed so that their long tails acts as propellants, and they will literally plant themselves when dropped to the ground by the wind. People would have certainly noticed that grain spilled around storage areas sprouted every spring. In countless ways nature offered her secrets to attentive man long before he tilled the earth. With this primitive, but basic, understanding of nature, the neolithic agricultural revolution began. Planting, fertilizing, irrigation, seed selection, and animal husbandry became a continuing way of life.

Once the basic principles of farming were developed, many plants could be added to the list of wheat, corn, rye, oats, and barley. Legumes of all kinds and nuts, along with the common garden plants, soon followed.

Animal husbandry and farming usually developed simultaneously, in mutual support and reliance. Man has lived long among the grazing animals, which he followed from grazing area to grazing area and killed what he required to survive. Some of these beasts were the ancestors of today's domesticated animals. Eventually, the thin line between following and herding disappeared. Domestication of animals already accustomed to man's presence was easily achieved. Since the first crops were grain, there was enough food for man and beast. Man ate the seeds, and the animals ate what was left, naturally fertilizing the ground as they grazed on the remaining stubble.

Perhaps the most complete study of man's transition from hunting and gathering to the life of settled farmers was carried out in the 1960s in the Tehuacan Valley in Mexico. Excavations in twelve different locations, including caves, uncovered over 100,000 plant specimens and 11,000 animal bones. When analyzed these specimens showed the gradual change in diet from hunted meat and gathered vegetables to food production in which new

plants were gradually introduced into cultivation. The time between 8000 and 2000 B.C. has been termed the food-collecting incipient cultivation period. The first crops to be developed in Latin America were bottle gourds, pumpkin, and chili peppers. Gourds were used as containers, pumpkin seed for food, and chili peppers for food and condiment. Pumpkin seeds contain all the essential amino acids; a 100-gram (3½-ounce) portion will provide the daily requirement of protein for an adult. By 2000 B.C. agriculture was advanced enough to make the subsequent civilizations of Mexico and Peru possible.

Indians have cultivated corn for more than 5,000 years. Ears of wild corn were originally about an inch long, but through selection the Indians developed corn into a staple food. Corn is low in the amino acid lysine but rich in methionine, while beans are rich in lysine and somewhat deficient in methionine. Eaten together in the form of tortillas and beans, they provide all the essential amino acids and can be used as a complete protein.

Archaeological studies done in Tamaulipas, Mexico, in the mid-1950s give a good picture of what the diet was like before the advent of agriculture and how the diet changed as agriculture became more and more successful. Before the cultivation of plants, about half the food eaten came from hunting and half from gathering plant foods. Just after cultivation began, food from hunting dropped to less than 20 percent of the total diet. The rest was made up of gathered plant foods. In 2000 B.C., when agriculture was well established, about 10 percent of the diet was from hunting, and about 50 percent from agriculture, and the remaining 40 percent from gathered plant foods. This pattern continued until around 700 A.D., when the hunting-based diet was increased to about 20 percent and plant food gathered and grown, was about 40 percent each. Perhaps cultivation took place because animals became scarce, or the existence of cultivated vegetable food sources made an alternative possible. But the fact remains, after agriculture the diet depended much less on animal protein.

Mexico is one area of the world where the development of agriculture did not go along with domestication of farm animals as a means of controlling the production of animal protein. The dog was domesticated, and the Mexican Hairless was raised for food along with domesticated turkeys. But, Latin America had to wait for the arrival of the Spaniards before the *major* sources of animal protein — cattle, pigs, goats, and sheep — were introduced into the diet. We can learn a good lesson from the early Latin Americans. Their lack of domesticated animals was not a lack of protein, for as early as 2000 B.C. beans and corn had been their major source of nourishment. The very high civilizations of the Aztecs, Incas, and Mayas flourished on a diet that was from 80 to 90 percent vegetable food.

THE ORIGINAL DIET

Man evolved for 150 million years on primarily a raw vegetarian diet. For approximately 149,500,000 years, or about 99 percent of that time, all food was eaten raw and in its natural state. Man's ancestors provided him with a system that is ideally suited to the digestion of raw fruits, vegetables, nuts and seeds — the original diet.

The jaws of lions, tigers, wolves, and other carnivores open and shut on a hinge. Their canine teeth are long and sharp; they tear off pieces of flesh and bolt them instead of chewing. Their intestinal tracts are only three times as long as their bodies. A short intestine is required to digest meat quickly so that the residue will not remain to putrify in the body any longer than necessary.

Grazing animals such as cattle, sheep, and horses have systems to process grasses and grains. Cattle have flat teeth and the jaw can move up, down and from side to side in a chewing, grinding motion. Their saliva is alkaline, which is best for the digestion of vegetable matter. Plant food does not putrify as readily as meat and can remain in the body longer, and additional time is needed to break down high-fiber-content food.

Most primates (which includes man, apes, and monkeys) are essentially frugivorous. Their teeth combine characteristics of the carnivore and the grazer; the canines are not so long as to interfere with the chewing motion of the flat molars. The saliva of primates is alkaline, and their intestinal tracts are about twelve times the length of the body. Meat will begin to putrify long before it passes through this lengthy system. Man's digestive system can handle small amounts of meat, but not well, since his saliva is alkaline instead of acid, and his intestinal tract is four times longer than a carnivore's. In addition, any parasites found in raw meat may be passed on to man.

We are fast raching the time when it will no longer be practical to convert grain protein into meat protein. About 3500 grams (*seven* pounds) of grain are needed to add 500 grams (*one* pound) of weight to a cow. For centuries man has depended on plant life to provide most of his protein requirements.

It has been argued that cooking provides us with food that would otherwise be inedible. Some seeds, such as legumes in their dry form, cause digestive problems. Legumes often cause gas and upset the digestive system even when cooked. However, when sprouted, many legumes (except soybeans) and dried seeds become excellent and easily digested vegetables.

We do not know how many nutrients are destroyed by cooking, because we do not know the complete chemical makeup of any food. According to the National Academy of Sciences:

> Many chemical components of natural food products have been identified. It is likely, however, that even more have not. The great number of chemical substances discovered in any single food study itself, reflect an almost endless variety of specific chemical compounds that remain to be discovered in the foods that make up the diet of man.

It is known, however, that enzymes and vitamin C are especially sensitive to heat. Roughage, nature's broom, becomes so soft in cooked foods that it does not do an effective job of cleaning and toning the intestines. If food is eaten raw, there is no fear of getting insufficient roughage in the diet. You only have to compare raw foods with cooked foods on a nutritional chart to realize how much known food value is lost through cooking.

The first food of all mammals is milk. But no animal except man continues to drink milk after it is weaned. Mother's milk is necessary to the growth of infants; it provides all the nourishment they need to begin life. Solid foods are added to the milk diet gradually, as the babies' teeth and digestive system continue to develop. Before the domestication of goats and cattle, milk was unavailable to man; therefore, it was not part of the original diet. The majority of the world's people develop early in life an intolerance to the principal sugar in cow's milk, lactose. For these people milk drinking can result in severe intestinal discomfort, including diarrhea, gas, and cramps.

Most Northern Europeans and Americans of Northern European ancestry are spared this distress.

Because milk from infected animals may contain harmful organisms such as tuberculosis or brucellosis (undulant fever), it is pasturized at temperatures up to 85° C. (185° F.). Sterilized milk is treated at temperatures as high as 135° C. (275° F.). Milk products such as curds and whey, buttermilk, yogurt, and kefir revitalize somewhat during fermentation. The high acid content of sour or fermented milk inhibits and often destroys many pathogenic bacterias, including typhoid and paratyphoid organisms. Also, noxious coliforms which cause intestinal diseases are less likely to occur with fermented milk products. (Tuberculosis and the brucellosis microorganisms cannot be controlled by souring the milk; the cow must be disease free.) Fermented milk products have a lower level of lactose; yogurt and other fermented milk foods are easier to digest than regular milk. In addition, yogurt helps prevent putrefaction in the large intestine. If any food of animal origin is included in the raw food diet, foods made from highly fermented milk are the best choice. A raw vegetarian purist would not use any milk products; but for a transitional diet, fermented milk products may prove helpful in satisfying the appetite and aiding a sluggish digestive system. Ultimately, when the body becomes accustomed to a diet almost entirely made up of raw fruits, vegetables, nuts, and grains, there is no need or appetite for fermented milk foods.

When fermented milk products are included in the diet, they should be made from high-quality milk. Cows fed with fodder that has been subjected to insecticides and herbicides may produce milk containing a residue of these chemicals, which pasturization does not eliminate. You can buy certified raw milk, available at most health food stores, and make your own fermented milk foods. Recipes for fermented milks are not included in this book. My book, *The Complete Yogurt Cookbook,* gives directions for making yogurt and provides many recipes that are suitable for a raw food diet.

Fermented foods such as cabbage (sauerkraut), green beans, beet tops, turnip tops, and olives are good sources of fresh, uncooked winter vegetables. Salt added to vegetables before fermenting will inhibit the development of toxin-producing microorganisms. Sugar, naturally present in vegetables, is fermented by the lactic-acid-forming bacteria present on the surface of fresh produce. When fermentation has reached a certain point, the food is preserved from further change as long as precautions are taken to prevent mold growth. Naturally fermented foods have been used as medicines for arthritis, scurvy, ulcers, colds, and digestive disorders. Any medicinal benefits may be attributed to the lactic acid and fermentive enzymes that are produced during fermentation. Lactic acid contributes to better digestion by creating an environment unfavorable to harmful intestinal bacteria. Fermented vegetables are also a good source of vitamin C. Commercially prepared fermented vegetables should not be eaten because they are made with vinegar and do not contain natural lactic acid. In addition, they are heated before canning. Fermented vegetables of any kind are high in sodium so use these products judiciously.

Before chickens were domesticated, man ate raw eggs only occasionally — when he could find them during the nesting season. Avidin, a substance in raw egg white, combines with the B vitamin, biotin, and prevents it from reaching the blood. Biotin deficiencies may cause nausea, vomiting, glossitis, depression, and dermatitis. Like milk, eggs may contain toxic residues from pesticides and herbicides. Chickens, chickenhouses, and chicken feed may have been subjected to pesticides and herbicides.

The original diet included a wide variety of fresh raw fruits, berries, vegetables, nuts seeds, grains, and, occasionally, meat. Honey and naturally dried fruits satisfied the desire for sweets. When concentrated forms of sugar are eaten the teeth should be brushed immediately afterward. Dried fruits and honey are concentrated forms of natural sugar, but can still cause tooth decay.

Raw plant food helps keep the digestive system strong and efficient. Since most people have eaten large amounts of cooked food most of their lives, their systems may have become sluggish on a soft diet. DO NOT change to a raw food diet too quickly. Digestive problems may arise if drastic food changes are suddenly made. Raw foods can be added to the diet gradually, just as a sedentary person begins physical exercise slowly.

A transitional diet containing some cooked fruits, vegetables, and grains is recommended. Nuts can be eaten raw. Meat may be excluded altogether without negative side effects, but if you wish to include some animal protein, you can use fermented milk products. Raw fruits and vegetables and other high fiber-content foods will not cause excess gas or diarrhea *if* they are increased gradually. Too much raw food at the beginning may interfere with the digestion and absorption of the nutrients of fruits and vegetables.

A few precautions will ensure maximum benefits from a raw vegetarian diet. First, be sure to eat more than one kind of vegetable protein at a meal. The body requires eight essential amino acids to break down and absorb protein: isoleucine, leucine, lysine, methionine, phenylalanine, threonine, tryptophan, and valine. The body needs many other amino acids, but it can manufacture them. Amino acids synthesized by the body are called "nonessential amino acids." The essential amino acids must be provided from food. A proper balance of amino acids in one food makes it a "complete protein." Most nuts, seeds, grains, and legumes contain all or many of the essential amino acids. The balance required to make full use of all the individual food protein is not always present; but if two or more vegetable proteins are eaten at the same meal, the chance of getting a correct balance is good. For example, Brazil nuts are low in lysine and high in methionine while cashews are low in methionine and high in lysine. When cashews *and* Brazil nuts are eaten at the same meal, a greater amount of protein from each can be utilized by the body. The *Nutrition Almanac* and *Diet for a Small Planet* (see bibliography) are helpful in selecting and balancing amino acids.

In *Let's Get Well* Adelle Davis wrote that total vegetarians are subject to pernicious anemia. Her reasoning is that the primary dietary sources of vitamin B-12 are meat, fish, poultry, eggs, and milk products. Vitamin B-12 is also synthesized by the intestinal tract bacteria in a healthy body. Davis, however, maintains that absorption from this source is doubtful since the intrinsic factor required to assimilate vitamin B-12 is produced in the stomach. The World Health Organization reports that dietary inadequacy of vitamin B-12 alone may cause mild deficiency symptoms, but rarely leads to pernicious anemia. The daily requirement for vitamin B-12 is about three micrograms. Small amounts of vitamin B-12 are found in sunflower seeds, comfrey leaves and roots, dehydrated alfalfa, and pollen. To avoid taking supplemental vitamins, one should be checked routinely for vitamin B-12 deficiency. It is possible that your system will produce and absorb all the required amount of vitamin B-12.

Dr. Harold Rosenburg warns that a total vegetarian may find his diet deficient in riboflavin (vitamin B-2). The daily requirement for an adult male is 1.6 milligrams per day, and for the adult female, 1.2 milligrams. A deficiency of vitamin B-2 can easily be avoided by including in daily meals foods rich in riboflavin such as almonds, Brazil nuts, pumpkin seeds, Brussels sprouts, asparagus, and avocadoes.

The same care should be exercised in a raw food diet as in any other diet to obtain a balance of all the nutrients the body requires. After being on a total raw food diet for a while, you will recognize cravings for certain foods as body signals for specific nutrients. A yearly checkup by a physician is also advisable, not just for people on a raw food diet but for everyone.

Even on a transitional diet there may be some occasional discomfort during the first weeks or months. Headaches, nausea, dizziness, tiredness, obscure aches and pains, and sleeplessness are not uncommon but they are usually short in duration and merely indicate that the system is going through a cleansing process. Every individual is different, so it is impossible to tell how long it will take the body to "clean house" and become accustomed to a total raw food diet. Persistent problems should be promptly referred to a physician.

Good health and good digestion are closely related. The number and types of food in a meal will determine how well each food is digested. Raw fruits require different enzymes for their digestion than those required for the digestion of raw vegetables. Dilute amounts of hydrochloric acid are needed to digest proteins, but the carbohydrates in fruits and vegetables inhibit the secretion of hydrochloric acid. If protein is eaten with other foods, eat the protein first. A very easy way to follow good food-combining rules is to eat one meal (for example, breakfast) of fruit, one meal (lunch) of nut, seed or grain protein; and one meal (dinner) of vegetables. A leafy salad could be eaten with the protein meal. There are no hard and fast rules about meal patterns. Generally, however, if the evening meal is small, sleep will be more relaxed and restful. Eat until just full. An overloaded digestive system is not only uncomfortable, it does not function efficiently.

If the food cannot be enjoyed it is best not to eat at all. Eating in a hurry or under stress causes indigestion. Chew food slowly and thoroughly. It may seem difficult, but one should chew solids until they are liquid and hold liquids in the mouth to mix with saliva as if they were solids. Drinking liquids with a meal may dilute the digestive juices; water or juices may be

taken twenty to thirty minutes before a meal without interfering with digestion. Eat foods you enjoy. There are so many plant foods to choose from that one can probably obtain a balanced diet without eating distasteful food.

The joys of having a healthy body cannot be overstated. Diet alone will not produce a healthy person. Good health and longevity depend on the inheritance of a strong body, eating a balance of nourishing unrefined foods, fresh air and sunshine, cleanliness, moderate exercise, and sufficient rest. A raw vegetarian diet is a most nourishing way to eat. After you have been on the diet for a while the whole body will feel lighter. Your joints will feel looser, you will feel more alert and energetic, more optimistic, and happier. You will have more energy and be less susceptible to disease. Some people require less sleep, some lose excess weight, and others experience a "spiritual high" after being on a raw vegetarian diet for a few months. Keep these benefits in mind when you are going through the transitional period. It is possible to have optimum health!

RAW FOOD AND SAVING ENERGY

The average homemaker spends a large part of life in the kitchen, cooking food and cleaning up after meals. Not so with raw vegetarian preparation. An estimated 90 kilograms (200 pounds) of airborn grease is released in the home every year. Some of it may go out the stove exhaust, but plenty is left to coat the walls, cupboards, floors, windows, hair, skin, and nasal passages. Much time, water, and polluting chemicals are required to remove it. Not cooking eliminates all 90 kilograms of grease.

Raw food is an energy saver. The average family in the United States uses 110 kilowatt hours per month for cooking. You would save about 1,300 kilowatt hours each year if you did not use your range and oven. Add up the national usage and the figures would be even more impressive. According to the December 1975 issue of *Ceres* magazine, one-third of the world's people search daily to find enough wood just to cook dinner. In Sahel, West Africa, the average manual laborer spends nearly one quarter of his income on firewood. In the United States, gas and electricity prices are steadily rising. By living on a raw diet, time is saved in food preparation and in cleanup after a meal. The time and physical energy saved by a raw vegetarian diet could be used to plant and maintain a garden of inexpensive organic fruits and vegetables.

FASTING

Fasting is as old as life. Nature has always had seasons of abundance and times of famine. The survival of a species may depend on its ability to live for long periods on limited or no food. Fasting is a natural, safe way for the body to metabolize its stored fat and protein to provide energy when food is not available. Some animals go into hibernation when food is scarce or unavailable. Bears, fat with plentiful summer food, sleep out the winter months, waking occasionally for drinks of water. By spring they are lean and hungry, ready to begin the cycle again. Female bears give birth during the winter and nurse their cubs, for even without food the mother bear's body is able to produce milk.

Animals self-impose a fast when sick or under stress. They drink only water, and the appetite does not return until the body is well enough to digest food properly. Man is the only animal that ignores this loss-of-appetite signal of illness or stress. Often people are urged to eat "to keep up your strength." Actually, eating may prolong illness. To keep the body at a peak of health periodic fasting seems to be natural. Dr. Alex Comfort, of London's University College, found that the life span of rats could be increased 50 percent by feeding only two days out of three. If this diet works as well for humans, the average Western woman could expect to live to 108 years.

Throughout history, man has undergone voluntary fasts for many reasons. Political protesters go on hunger strikes to draw attention to their cause. Some Indian tribes fasted before setting out for hunts. Fasting has been used for thousands of years as a means of attaining a higher state of consciousness. Fasts are routinely used in many religions. The Zen-Avesta religion recommends a fast every fifth day. Syrians fast every seventh and Mongolians every tenth day. Jesus fasted for forty days; and Moses and Elijah also fasted.

Fasting has been used to overcome intestinal disorders and obesity. From a biochemical point of view, total fasting is the most efficient way to lose weight. The body fat is consumed as the main source of energy for the brain and other tissues. Long fasts — up to 249 days — have been undergone by obese persons to lose weight. These fasts were carried out in hospitals and monitored by physicians. No harmful side effects were suffered because of the lack of food. Some doctors feel that several short fasts, evenly spaced at intervals, can be as effective as one long one. Others prefer to conduct juice fasts rather than total fasts.

Dr. H. M. Shelton believes that fasting is an excellent way to revitalize the body. His reasoning is that toxic materials are stored in the fat when the body is unable to eliminate them. When one fasts, the cells are able to remove the stored foreign substances. The cells again become youthful and function more efficiently.

A short fast is helpful before starting a raw vegetarian diet or, for that matter, any diet different from the one to which you are accustomed. During a fast the entire eating pattern is broken, after which it is easier to change eating habits. Many people find they prefer fresh raw fruits and vegetables after fasting. It must be emphasized that one should not undertake fasting without prior medical advice. Fasting is not for everyone. It is not advisable for people with a history of cardiovascular diseases, liver diseases, or gout. Children cannot fast for long. Their growing bodies need constant supplies of building materials. Inadequate nutrition can cause permanent brain or bone damage.

In most cases, healthy adults will have no difficulty with a few days' abstention from food, and will most likely find the experience rewarding enough to repeat at intervals for the rest of their lives. Some possible discomforts to anticipate during a fast are coated tongue, nausea, and headaches. Sip water for the nausea, take an enema for the headache, and gently clean the tongue with water and a soft toothbrush a few times a day. Avoid too much exercise, even during a short fast. Some people experience light-headedness when rising from a reclining or sitting position. This can be avoided by rising slowly.

26

Breaking a fast should be done gradually on light foods such as fresh vegetable juices. Celery juice is a good starter. The next meal may be a small, leafy, green salad with lemon juice *only* — no salt or oil. Never break a fast on concentrated sweets such as dried fruits, or low-water-content foods such as nuts, grains, and legumes. Long fasts should be done under the supervision of a physician and broken as he recommends. It takes a while for the digestive system to return to full efficiency after a fast.

If you are contemplating a fast you will find that books on the subject can be very helpful, interesting, and encouraging. Several books are devoted exclusively to fasting and many more include a chapter or two on the subject. There is a list of books about fasting at the end of this book.

Your attitude toward a fast is important. Select a time for fasting when you are not under more than normal stress or physical activity. There will be fewer ill effects when you are confident and free from anxiety. Fasting can be an adventure that will teach you to be more aware of your body. With a doctor's approval, the mind can rest as easily as the body and the fast can be a satisfying and rewarding experience.

SODIUM

Sodium is a necessary mineral in the human diet. It is found in virtually all foods, so table salt (sodium chloride) need rarely be added to food for the sake of health. Vegetables rich in sodium are wheat, rye, bananas, celery, dandelion greens, lettuce, spinach, sweet potato, beets, watercress, mushrooms, carrots, and kelp.

The daily dietary requirement of sodium has not been established, but it is generally agreed that the intake of the average person in modern industrial society is far in excess of the need. Any excess sodium must be either eliminated or tolerated by the body. An inability to tolerate excessive amounts of salt may cause side effects such as elevated blood pressure, aggravated kidney disorders, rheumatic swellings, skin problems, and edema (water retention). Excess sodium interferes with the absorption and utilization of nutrients, especially protein, and hinders the elimination of uric acid.

In correct doses sodium relaxes muscles and, together with potassium, maintains a perfect balance of water retention for health. Salt taken in excess may promote heavy kidney loss of potassium. The small amount required for good health can be obtained from vegetables, fruits, and seeds. There is no danger of excess sodium in the diet when it is obtained from plant food.

Recipes in this book do not include salt. If salt is added for flavor, use sea salt, which contains some calcium, magnesium, carbon, sulphur, potassium, and about thirty other trace minerals. Sea salt should be used sparingly, since any excess will be a burden on the body. Delicious salt substitutes are ground kelp and ground garden cress seed, which contain natural sodium and other valuable minerals. Garden cress seed and kelp can be used freely.

VEGETABLE OILS

A wide variety of natural oils (that is, mildly processed) can be found in a well-stocked health food store, including olive, peanut, corn, sesame, soybean, almond, apricot, pumpkin, sunflower, rice brand, walnut, safflower, and avocado oil. They may be labeled cold pressed, but none of these oils are raw.

Oils are extracted in one of two ways: mechanical expression or solvent extraction. Mechanical expression includes hydraulic press and expeller, or screw-type, press. Both generate heat during processing and the temperature of the oil may rise between 52°C. (130°F.) and 63°C. (150°F.) even under the best conditions. Heating frees the oil and it destroys a digestion-inhibiting substance in soybeans. Heavily processed oils (refined, deodorized, and bleached) may have been subjected to temperatures as high as 228°C. before they are bottled. In solvent extraction, the oil-bearing matter is heated, treated with dissolving chemicals, then heated again to remove the solvents. The solvents leave a dry residue, part of which may remain in the oil. Nutritionist Linda Clark believes that solvent-extracted oil should not be used for human consumption.

If extracted oils are included in your diet, buy those that have been subjected to the least abuse. These are the cold-pressed oils. Cold press means that the oil-bearing material has not been heated before extraction. Cold-pressed oil should be crude, virgin, unrefined oil to which no preservatives have been added. Such natural oils still contain chlorophyll, lecithin, vitamin E, carotenoids, and minerals such as copper, calcium, magnesium, and iron. Buy cold-pressed oils in small quantities and store in the refrigerator to preserve freshness.

Heavily refined oils are not only heated at high temperatures, they have also been chemically refined to eliminate flavor, odor, and color (flour is refined for the same reason). Very little is left in heavily processed oils except their lubricating quality.

If your goal is to avoid all cooked and chemically processed foods, then *all* bottled oil must be eliminated from your diet. One source of raw oil is found floating on top of raw nut and seed butters. You can skim small amounts of pure oil from the top of the butter as you would cream from a bottle of raw milk. The remaining butter is still tasty without excessive oil. Ground raw nuts and seeds are excellent replacements for oil in salad dressings and sauces. If you grind your own seeds and nuts, nothing is lost and the product is as fresh as the nuts or seeds used. Ground nuts and seeds should be refrigerated if not used immediately.

FRUITS

Fully ripened fruits are sweeter, more appetizing, more satisfying, more digestible, and have more nutrients than immature ones. The best fruits are ripened on the tree or vine, but unless you grow your own it is virtually impossible to eat only tree or vine-ripened fruits. Ripe fruits contain more fruit sugar than green ones. For example, green bananas contain 2 percent fruit sugar, compared to 20 percent when ripe.

Because fruits are alive, they are affected by the atmosphere around them. Most tropical fruits, if picked green, will not ripen if they have been ·chilled at temperatures lower than 12° C. (55° F.). If fruits such as bananas avocados, papayas, mangoes, and pineapples fail to ripen at room temperature, return them to the grocer. They were probably chilled during shipping or storage. Many fruits will not continue to develop their fruit sugar after picking; they may soften but they will not ripen. These fruits should be brought at the ready-to-eat ripeness. Buy fruit that is ripe but firm; overly ripe fruit spoils quickly. Avoid fruit with soft spots or bruises. Fruit that is to be ripened at home should already have some color. Mangoes and pineapples, for example, if completely green, will not ripen properly. Store fully ripened fruit unwashed in the refrigerator. Bananas are an exception, for their flavor is affected if chilled. Fruit that is not fully ripe can be ripened at room temperature and then be refrigerated unwashed.

FRUIT RIPENING CHART

Fruits that will not ripen after picking	*Fruits that will continue to ripen at room temperature*
All apples except Yellow Delicious and Gravenstein	Apples, Yellow Delicious and Gravenstein
Berries	Avocados
Cherries	Apricots
Citrus fruits	Bananas
Figs	Carambola (star fruit)
Grapes	Cherimoya
Melons	Guava
Nectarines	Kivi
Peaches	Mangoes
	Papayas
	Pears
	Persimmons
	Pineapple
	Plums
	Pomegranates
	Prickley pear
	Sapote (custard apple)

VEGETABLES

There are three separate edible parts of vegetables: the plant, the fruit, and the root. The plant includes its leaves, stalk, and flowers. The fruit includes the seed, seed pod, and the fleshy fruit. The root is the part growing underground and includes bulbs and rizomes. Sprouts are also classified as vegetables.

When buying vegetables, be very critical. Inspect vegetables carefully and choose only those that are crisp, plump, and fresh. Brown spots indicate that decay has begun. Limp vegetables have lost some of their moisture, along with some of their flavor and nutrients. Find out what days your favorite store has produce deliveries and try to pick up the most perishable vegetables on those days.

Store leafy greens, such as spinach, lettuce, and collards, in the vegetable crisper or in a plastic bag. Do not wash before storing. It is almost impossible to wash leafy vegetables without damaging them. Broken vegetable skins and excess moisture invite an invasion of microorganisms which can cause the plant to decay quickly. Just before using, rinse vegetable greens thoroughly, drain or dry gently with a terrycloth towel or paper towel. The leaves of plants are usually its most perishable part. They should be used as soon as possible after purchase. Broccoli, cauliflower, celery, cabbage and Brussels sprouts will keep somewhat longer.

With the exception of the hard-shell squash family, root vegetables are the best keepers of the three categories. Roots may be rinsed before storing, but they should not be scrubbed until just before they are used. Brushing cleans the roots thoroughly but also breaks the skin, allowing water loss and decay to start. A nylon brush is handy for cleaning root vegetables. Vegetable fruits and roots may be washed with a mild organic soap and rinsed thoroughly.

The fruits of vegetables includes beans, eggplants, pumpkins, tomatoes, zucchini, okra, peppers, peas, and squash. They should be used as soon as possible, since they do not keep as well as roots. Store vegetable fruits unwashed in the refrigerator in plastic bags or in a vegetable crisper. Eggplant should not be refrigerated since they should not be chilled at lower than 10°C. (50°F.).

PRODUCE CALENDAR

Listed below are many of the fruits and vegetables found in super-markets. You can usually buy the best quality when the greatest quantity is available, that is, in season. Fruits and vegetables are shipped by truck, train, boat, and airplane. Some are imported from as near as Mexico or as far away as China and New Zealand. As a result of importing produce, some fruits and vegetables can be bought the year around. However, the cost of shipping is reflected in the market price.

AVERAGE MONTHLY AVAILABILITY OF FRESH
FRUITS & VEGETABLES

MONTHLY AVAILABILITY EXPRESSED AS PERCENTAGE OF TOTAL ANNUAL SUPPLY

COMMODITY	Jan. %	Feb. %	Mar. %	Apr. %	May %	June %	July %	Aug. %	Sept. %	Oct. %	Nov. %	Dec. %	ANNUAL TOTAL million lbs.
APPLES, all	10	9	10	9	8	5	3	4	9	12	10	11	3,470
" Washington	10	11	11	11	11	7	4	2	5	8	9	11	1,580
" New York	10	10	12	11	9	6	2	2	7	11	10	10	375
" Michigan	13	12	12	10	6	2	*	2	5	13	12	13	260
" California	6	6	7	5	2	1	4	15	26	15	8	5	152
" Virginia	9	8	8	5	2	*	1	2	16	19	17	13	138
APRICOTS					11	60	27	2					24
ARTICHOKES	4	6	14	19	12	5	6	7	5	8	8	6	68
ASPARAGUS	*	6	28	31	20	10	*	*	1	1	1		100
AVOCADOS, all	9	7	8	8	8	7	7	8	7	9	11	11	170
" California	7	8	11	10	10	10	8	8	6	6	8	8	127
BANANAS	8	8	10	9	8	8	7	7	7	8	9	9	3,845
BEANS, SNAP, all	6	4	6	9	10	12	12	11	9	8	7	6	338
" Florida	12	9	14	20	14	3	*		*	2	12	14	134
BEETS	5	5	6	6	6	12	14	13	12	10	7	4	27
BERRIES, MISC. **					2	30	39	14	8	5	2		4
BLUEBERRIES					1	26	43	28	2				33
BROCCOLI	10	9	12	9	9	7	5	5	7	9	9	9	102
BRUSSELS SPROUTS	13	13	12	7	4	*		2	6	14	17	12	20

Reprinted by permission of the United Fresh Fruit and Vegetable Association, Washington, D.C. 20036.

MONTHLY AVAILABILITY EXPRESSED AS PERCENTAGE OF TOTAL ANNUAL SUPPLY

COMMODITY	Jan. %	Feb. %	Mar. %	Apr. %	May %	June %	July %	Aug. %	Sept. %	Oct. %	Nov. %	Dec. %	ANNUAL TOTAL million lbs.
CABBAGE, all	**10**	**8**	**9**	**9**	**9**	**9**	**8**	**7**	**7**	**8**	**8**	**8**	**1,900**
" Florida	17	15	19	22	15	3	*			*	1	8	415
" Texas	16	14	18	12	8	3	2	2	1	3	8	13	355
" California	10	9	11	9	11	11	7	6	5	7	7	7	252
" New York	9	7	5	3	1	1	7	10	12	16	17	12	159
" North Carolina	1			*	11	27	9	10	9	8	17	8	102
CANTALOUPES, all		*	**3**	**4**	**10**	**20**	**25**	**22**	**11**	**4**	**1**		**1,410**
" California					*	15	28	33	16	6	1	*	855
" Mexico		1	17	32	43	7							212
" Texas					23	47	19	9	1	*			158
" Arizona					*	48	47	*		4	*		98
CARROTS, all	**10**	**9**	**10**	**9**	**8**	**7**	**7**	**7**	**7**	**9**	**9**	**8**	**1,455**
" California	9	8	8	8	10	11	11	8	6	6	7	8	879
" Texas	15	16	18	16	8	3	*	2	2	3	7	9	283
CAULIFLOWER, all	**9**	**6**	**8**	**7**	**6**	**6**	**5**	**6**	**9**	**15**	**14**	**9**	**165**
" California	10	7	10	10	9	8	6	6	6	8	10	10	115
CELERY, all	**9**	**8**	**9**	**8**	**8**	**8**	**8**	**7**	**7**	**8**	**10**	**10**	**1,548**
" California	8	6	7	7	7	10	9	7	7	9	13	10	1,041
" Florida	15	15	17	15	14	8	1			*	3	11	371
" Michigan						1	20	29	30	16	3	1	66
CHERRIES, SWEET					**11**	**41**	**43**	**5**					**123**
CHINESE CABBAGE	**10**	**9**	**8**	**8**	**8**	**8**	**7**	**8**	**8**	**9**	**9**	**8**	**53**
COCONUTS	**9**	**7**	**9**	**7**	**6**	**5**	**4**	**7**	**8**	**8**	**11**	**19**	**26**
CORN, SWEET, all	**3**	**2**	**4**	**7**	**16**	**17**	**16**	**14**	**8**	**5**	**5**	**3**	**1,600**
" Florida	5	4	6	11	27	24	5	*	*	5	7	6	850
" California					10	27	25	17	9	7	4	*	174
" New York							5	45	40	10			97
CRANBERRIES									**8**	**26**	**48**	**18**	**38**
CUCUMBERS, all	**7**	**5**	**6**	**7**	**11**	**12**	**12**	**9**	**8**	**8**	**8**	**7**	**664**
" Florida	4	1	2	10	29	11	1		*	7	21	13	180
" Mexico	23	21	23	15	2	*					2	13	127
" California	*	*	1	3	12	15	21	17	13	10	6	2	75
EGGPLANT	**10**	**8**	**8**	**9**	**7**	**7**	**8**	**10**	**9**	**8**	**8**	**8**	**100**
ESCAROLE-ENDIVE	**10**	**9**	**10**	**10**	**9**	**8**	**7**	**7**	**6**	**7**	**8**	**9**	**160**
GARLIC	**8**	**8**	**8**	**8**	**8**	**8**	**10**	**9**	**10**	**9**	**7**	**6**	**25**
GRAPEFRUIT, all	**12**	**12**	**12**	**11**	**10**	**6**	**4**	**3**	**3**	**8**	**10**	**9**	**1,857**
" Florida	11	12	13	13	11	5	2	*	3	10	10	10	1,270
" Texas	18	18	18	11	4	*			*	5	11	14	340
" Western	5	5	6	7	12	15	17	16	10	2	2	3	242

MONTHLY AVAILABILITY EXPRESSED AS PERCENTAGE OF TOTAL ANNUAL SUPPLY

COMMODITY	Jan. %	Feb. %	Mar. %	Apr. %	May %	June %	July %	Aug. %	Sept. %	Oct. %	Nov. %	Dec. %	ANNUAL TOTAL million lbs.
GRAPES	4	3	3	3	2	6	11	17	18	15	10	8	474
GREENS***	10	9	11	10	9	7	6	6	7	8	8	9	250
HONEY DEWS	1	1	3	5	7	12	10	20	22	15	3	1	310
LEMONS	8	6	8	8	9	11	11	9	7	8	7	8	420
LETTUCE, all	8	7	9	9	9	9	9	9	8	8	8	7	4,620
" California	8	8	8	7	10	10	10	9	9	9	7	5	3,367
" Arizona	11	6	13	25	7	1	*	*	*	2	13	21	600
" Florida	16	15	20	16	9	*				*	8	15	91
" Ohio	6	6	9	7	6	8	12	12	9	9	9	7	83
LIMES	6	4	5	5	9	12	13	12	10	8	7	9	38
MANGOS	*	1	3	6	17	23	28	17	4	1			24
MUSHROOMS	9	8	9	9	9	8	7	7	7	8	9	9	73
NECTARINES	*	*	*		1	19	36	30	12	*			160
OKRA	2	3	6	7	11	14	17	17	11	7	3	2	39
ONIONS, DRY, all	9	7	8	8	9	9	9	9	8	9	8	7	2,000
" Texas	1	*	4	26	27	14	12	10	3	1	1	1	443
" California	3	1	1	1	11	21	23	17	8	6	5	3	329
" New York	12	9	11	6	2	1	1	8	14	13	12	11	256
ONIONS, GREEN	7	6	8	10	11	10	10	8	7	7	7	7	178
ORANGES, all	11	12	13	11	10	7	5	4	4	5	8	10	3,240
" Western	9	10	12	12	11	7	5	5	6	6	7	10	2,063
" Florida	14	15	14	11	9	6	3	1	1	4	9	13	998
PAPAYAS, HAWAII	6	6	6	7	10	10	9	8	8	10	11	9	27
PARSLEY & HERBS***	8	7	9	7	7	8	7	8	8	9	11	11	83
PARSNIPS	12	11	11	9	7	5	3	4	8	11	10	9	25
PEACHES, all	*	*			6	17	31	29	15	1			1,020
" California					8	22	34	24	10	2			287
" South Carolina					1	19	53	26	1				220
" Georgia					5	42	45	8					135
" New Jersey						8	54	37	1				128
PEARS, all	7	7	7	6	4	2	4	13	16	17	10	7	490
" California	1	*	*	*			12	33	27	20	5	1	153
" Washington	9	9	8	6	2			9	16	16	14	11	141
" Oregon	16	16	13	7	1			*	3	15	16	13	137
PEAS, GREEN	12	12	13	13	12	12	10	6	5	2	1	2	18
PEPPERS, all	8	7	8	7	8	10	11	9	9	8	8	7	558
" Florida	15	9	10	14	16	14	1			*	6	15	165
" California			*	2	7	13	15	20	28	14	1		100
" Mexico	19	24	25	13	5	2	1	1	1	1	2	6	95

34

MONTHLY AVAILABILITY EXPRESSED AS PERCENTAGE OF TOTAL ANNUAL SUPPLY

COMMODITY	Jan. %	Feb. %	Mar. %	Apr. %	May %	June %	July %	Aug. %	Sept. %	Oct. %	Nov. %	Dec. %	ANNUAL TOTAL million lbs.
PERSIMMONS										33	48	19	5
PINEAPPLES	7	7	11	10	12	12	9	7	6	5	7	7	178
PLANTAINS	7	7	6	8	8	9	9	11	10	9	6	10	97
PLUMS-PRUNES	*	*	*		1	15	33	32	15	2			280
POMEGRANATES								2	9	72	15	2	10
POTATOES, all	9	8	9	8	9	8	8	8	8	9	8	8	11,725
" California	5	5	5	4	9	23	23	9	5	4	4	4	1,793
" Idaho	13	12	13	13	13	7	1	*	1	6	10	10	1,534
" Maine	13	12	15	17	15	5	*	*	1	3	8	10	1,194
" Colorado	12	10	12	11	7	*	*	6	9	11	10	11	746
" North Dakota	15	13	14	12	5	1	*	*	2	9	14	14	727
PUMPKINS	1	1	2	2	2	2	*	*	3	83	2	1	50
RADISHES	8	8	10	11	11	8	8	7	6	6	9	8	243
RHUBARB	8	15	16	23	21	9	3	1	1	1	1	1	15
SPINACH, all	9	9	11	9	9	8	7	6	7	8	8	9	61
" California	9	10	12	10	9	7	7	7	6	7	8	8	24
SQUASH, all	8	6	6	7	8	9	10	9	9	11	10	7	376
" California	4	3	3	8	10	12	11	10	10	13	11	5	97
" Florida	11	9	11	15	15	3	*	1	1	6	14	14	73
STRAWBERRIES, all	3	5	8	18	29	16	7	5	4	2	1	2	372
" California		*	3	22	35	18	9	6	4	2	*	*	275
" Mexico	21	25	29	5						*	5	14	58
SWEETPOTATOES, all	9	8	8	7	5	3	3	5	9	11	19	13	854
" North Carolina	9	8	10	10	7	4	1	1	6	12	19	13	252
" Louisiana	9	8	9	6	2	*	5	11	11	11	16	12	211
" California	8	7	8	8	5	4	3	3	7	10	20	17	143
TANGELOS	23	4	*							*	33	39	142
TANGERINES	21	8	7	4	2	*			*	5	20	32	270
TOMATOES, all	7	6	8	8	11	11	11	9	7	8	7	7	2,530
" California	1	*		*	1	8	17	16	16	22	13	5	798
" Mexico	13	17	22	20	16	5	*	*	*	*	2	3	638
" Florida	14	8	10	12	20	13	*	*		*	6	17	630
" Ohio			1	6	18	20	24	11	5	6	7	2	80
TURNIPS & RUTABAGAS	12	10	10	8	6	4	4	6	7	11	13	9	186
" Canada	11	10	9	7	3	1	1	4	10	12	19	13	70
WATERMELONS	*	*	1	3	10	28	31	20	5	1	*	*	2,860

* Supply is less than 0.5% of annual total.
** Mostly raspberries, blackberries and dewberries.
*** Includes kale, kohlrabi, collards, cabbage sprouts, dandelion, mustard and turnip tops, poke salad, bok choy and rappini.
**** Includes also parsley root, anise, basil, chives, dill, horseradish and others.

NUTS, GRAINS, AND SEEDS

Because there are so many kinds of seeds, nuts, and grains, it would be difficult to become bored with a diet relying on them for protein. And since they should be combined for higher protein utilization, the flavor variety becomes even greater. Many nuts and seeds contain more protein, ounce for ounce, than meat, and they are a good source of vitamins, minerals, and unsaturated oils. The shell also protects the nut meat from insecticides.

There is a danger in eating foods with high oil content if the oil has turned rancid. Rancidity is caused by oxidation of the oil, which can come about through prolonged storage or storage at too-high temperatures. Oxidation produces chemical substances which, when eaten, irritate the lining of the stomach and interfere with digestion by retarding the pancreatic enzymes. Consumption of rancid oil can also cause destruction of stored vitamins A, E, and F in the body.

Nuts and seeds mature in the fall, and many unhulled nuts and seeds will keep a full year in good condition. But shelled nuts and seeds, especially broken or damaged ones, deteriorate quickly. Sesame seeds, which are 60 percent oil, can become rancid in only six months even when properly stored.

The best way to ensure having a supply of fresh nuts and seeds is to buy in the fall or early in their season, then store in air-tight containers in a cool, dark place. Sesame seeds, Brazil nuts, sunflower seeds, flax seeds, cashews, and other highly perishable nuts and seeds should be frozen until needed. Never buy broken or damaged nuts and seeds; they may be rancid before you bring them home.

Grains are generally hardier than nuts and oil-rich seeds. They should be stored in a cool, dry, dark place and milled just before using. Milled wheat germ is highly perishable and should not be bought unless milled within the week of use. Fresh wheat germ has a sweet flavor; rancid wheat germ tastes bitter. Freeze wheat germ if you buy more than can be immediately used. Grains, nuts, and seeds are low-moisture-content foods that freeze well. Nature often freezes seeds during the winter months as they lie on or in the ground. Freezing does not prevent sprouting after the spring thaw.

SPROUTS

The raw food vegetarian can make better use of legumes and grains by sprouting them. A dry seed may contain as little as 12 percent water, but sprouted it may contain as much as 95 percent. The increased moisture makes the seed easier to digest. Sprouts are among the healthiest food available. Rich in vitamins, minerals, and protein, yet low in calories and cost, sprouts provide a constant supply of fresh vegetables even during the most severe winters.

When buying seeds for sprouting, select only those sold for growing purposes. Only untreated seeds should be used. Seeds sold for planting may have been treated with an insecticide-fungicide mixture to prevent or reduce losses caused by organisms associated with the seed or present in the soil. Legumes and grains found in food markets, unless otherwise labeled, are food-quality seeds. They are sold for cooking, and may be dead and therefore will not sprout. Most health food stores stock grains, nuts, and legumes suitable for sprouting. Viable, untreated garden and herb seed can be obtained from seed companies such as W. Atlee Burpee Co. and Ferry-Morse Seed Co. Be sure to specify *untreated seeds* when ordering by mail.

When buying seeds in a store, inspect them carefully to make certain they are in good condition. Seeds should be unbroken, without discoloration, missing embryos, or other damage. Experiment with a small amount of seed before investing in a few months' supply.

Seeds that produce a noxious plant should not be sprouted for food. Potato, tomato, and lupine are poisonous in plant form.

Harvest grain seeds when the root is the length of the seed. Alfalfa sprouts should be 25 to 50 millimeters (1 to 2 inches) long. Mung bean sprouts are ready to eat when they are 50 to 75 millimeters (2 to 3 inches) long. Lentils are best at about 25 millimeters, and soybeans and peas should be 50 millimeters long.

The time required for growing sprouts depends on the air temperature and the type of seed. Sunflower seeds sprout in 24 to 36 hours, and develop a tangy taste if the sprout exceeds the length of the seed. Alfalfa sprouts and other small seeds will sprout within 3 to 5 days. Grains require 3 to 5 days of germination.

The seed coats of beans and peas are usually tough but can be easily removed when rinsing. Most of the hulls will float to the top of the water. The seed coats of small seeds such as alfalfa can be removed in this way, or they can be eaten.

Before storing, let sprouts drain three or four hours after the last rinse. They will keep better without excess moisture. Store sprouts loosely in sealed glass jars or covered plastic containers. Plastic bags are not recommended since the tender sprouts are easily crushed, and damaged sprouts decay quickly. Grain sprouts should be stored in the coldest part of the refrigerator (about 2° C., or 35° F.) because some types continue to grow even after refrigeration. Many sprouts will stay crisp a week or more, but like any vegetable, the fresher they are, the more flavor and food value they contain.

How to Sprout Seeds

Equipment:

Widemouth jar
Cheesecloth, nylon net, nylon stocking, or plastic screen
Rubber band, jar cap ring, or string

Approximate yield:

½ cup beans makes 3 cups of sprouts
½ cup grain seed makes 2½ cups of sprouts
½ cup alfalfa seed makes 4 to 5 cups of sprouts

Measure seeds and pick over them carefully, retaining only whole seeds for sprouting. Broken seeds are likely to ferment. Wash seeds well and place them in a bowl or jar with lukewarm water, using four cups of water for one cup of seeds, to soak overnight. Drain. (Alfalfa seeds do not require presoaking.)

Place presoaked seeds in the sprouting jar, which should be large enough to allow for seed growth and air circulation (presoaking can be done directly in the jar). Cover the jar opening with a piece of cheesecloth, nylon net, or nylon stocking; hold in place with a rubber band, string, or jar cap ring. A piece of plastic screen cut to fit inside a jar cap ring also works well. Rinse and drain seeds two to four times a day, depending on the type of seed and the weather. Small seeds cling together, holding the moisture, and need not be rinsed as often as large seeds like beans, which tend to ferment easily and should be rinsed four times a day. For most seeds, a rinse in the morning and again at night is enough to maintain a moist atmosphere. In warm, dry weather, the water may evaporate more quickly and require additional rinsings.

Cover the jar with a brown paper bag if you plan to leave the jar out in the light. Light inhibits the development of vitamin C in some types of seeds. Lay the jar in a bowl, mouth down at a slight angle. Be sure the angle is not so severe that the seeds fall to the mouth of the jar, cutting off air circulation. The best temperature for sprouting most seeds is between 18° and 24° C. (65° to 75° F.). However, wheat and rye will sprout at temperatures as low as 5° C.

When the sprouts are the desired length, remove the paper bag and put the jar, uncovered, in the light to "green" the leaf sprouts. This takes only a few hours in indirect sunlight. Sunflower seeds, grains, and mung bean sprouts are tastier "ungreened." Leaf-type sprouts have far more chlorophyll and a better flavor when the leaves are a deep green.

My book, *The Complete Sprouting Cookbook,* provides further special instructions and tips for sprouting individual kinds of seeds. The book also includes many recipes using sprouts that are suitable for the raw food diet.

DEHYDRATION OF PRODUCE

Foods may be preserved by canning, freezing, fermenting, and drying. Of these methods, drying is the most natural, the least expensive, and the simplest. Properly dried foods retain their color, flavor, food value, and aroma better than food preserved by other methods. Dried foods require less room for storage, and if stored correctly can be kept until the next season. Most important, produce can be dried at low temperatures so that it remains raw.

Nature dries grains, nuts, and seeds to preserve them until weather conditions are favorable for sprouting. Grapes will dry on the vine, producing sun-dried raisins. Prehistoric man and animals survived on dried foods such as seeds, berries, and fodders of all kinds. Neandertal man had caches which included dried foods. American Indians were sun-drying corn, berries, nuts, meat, and fish long before the pilgrims founded Plymouth Colony.

Many animals collect and store dried foods for winter use. Some gather moist foods and sun-dry them before storage. Squirrels have been known to spread mushrooms along branches of trees for drying in the sun. Kangaroo rats collect green seeds during the spring months when plentiful. The immature seeds are buried in shallow beds and covered with a layer of soil so the sun will warm and dry them. After they are thoroughly dried, the rats dig up the seeds in the fall and store them for winter use. Bees concentrate their honey by fanning their wings; excess moisture is carried away by warm circulating air. Sealed vessels of honey removed from the ancient Egyptian tombs were found to be as good and fragrant as fresh honey.

Modern man has devised many techniques for drying food. Most commercially dried foods are either sulphured or blanched before being dried at high temperatures. Sulphuring prevents oxidation of fruits, thereby preserving the color and vitamins A and C. Unfortunately, it leaves a residue of sulphur odor and taste. Sulphur also destroys enzymes. Blanching partially cooks food and in doing so alters the flavor, deactivates enzymes, and many of the heat-sensitive vitamins are lost. For a raw food vegetarian the most desirable method of drying produce is to dry the food as naturally and as quickly as possible at temperatures under 53° C. (125° F.). Under these conditions the moisture will be removed without disturbing the vitamins and enzymes. Moisture will reactivate the enzyme action after the food is reconstituted with water. The food should then be used immediately.

Drying Equipment

The primary prerequisite of food drying is well-circulated, warm, dry air, which can be found in several ways: in a warm room or attic, out-of-doors in the sun, or in a home dehydrator. If you are fortunate enough to live in one of the few areas where one can depend on several days of low humidity, sunshine, and a nice breeze, sun-drying is possible. If you have a warm attic and a fan to circulate the air and keep it under $53°$ C., then you have a ready-made dehydrator. Be sure to check the attic temperature on one of the hottest days, as it is not unusual for attics to exceed $53°$ C. In a warm room one can hang string beans, chili peppers, garlic, and onions. Bunches of herbs also dry well.

Though expensive, a dehydrator takes the guesswork out of drying and consistently produces a good product. The expense is well worth while if you have access to a large supply of inexpensive produce during the summer. In an area where fresh produce is scarce or of poor quality during the winter, a dehydrator would be a good investment. Many companies demonstrate their dryers at county fairs and in department stores. It is best to see and taste the results of a dehydrator before buying. Make sure you buy one with an adjustable thermostat to regulate the temperature. It must also have a fan to circulate the air evenly throughout the box. The vents should be sufficient to remove the moist air so the drying time will be short. The best dehydrators will dry each shelf evenly so that it is not necessary to rotate them. The frame of the tray should be strong and the covering either polymer (Teflon) coated fiber or stainless steel mesh. Wooden trays are also acceptable, but they are very difficult to keep clean.

Sun-drying is more difficult because one has so little control over the many climatic variables. The best weather for drying is several warm days in succession with low humidity and a slight breeze. The drying trays should be made of the same materials as in the dehydrator; never use aluminum as it may chemically react with some produce, causing discoloration. Trays with widely spaced slats may be used if covered with a piece of cheesecloth to prevent the food from falling through as it shrinks. Roasting racks or oven trays work well. Sun-drying produces a darker produce than a dehydrator. Some fruits such as apples, peaches, pears, apricots and nectarines require treatment to preserve the color when sun-dried. This treatment can be a natural dip of water and lemon juice, ascorbic acid, salt, vinegar, or honey. Salt adds sodium to the diet and honey extends the drying time because of added sugar. When sun-drying use cheesecloth over the food to keep off insects. Bring the trays in each night to prevent the drying food from reabsorbing moisture from the night air.

The quality of the dried food will depend largely on the quality of the fresh product. Choose produce that is at ready-to-eat ripeness. Avoid bruised produce, which will darken as it dries. If possible buy produce grown without chemicals. Otherwise wash the fruits and vegetables with cool water and a biodegradable soap. Wax and oil on commercial produce can be removed by washing in warm soapy water and rinsing well.

Prepare the produce as you would for eating. Handle the food carefully to prevent bruising. Wash it, then dry off the excess water with paper or cloth towels. Remove pits, stems, and any imperfections. To prevent discoloration use only stainless steel cutting blades. With a large quantity of food, a small hand-operated slicer will make the work go faster, and will cut the produce in uniform slices that will dry evenly. Fruit should be cut into quarter-inch slices. Vegetables will dry faster than fruit because of their low sugar content, but for the best product cut them into quarter-inch slices also. Onions and celery are exceptions and may be cut one-third to one-half-inch thick and still yield a good product. There is no need to peel fruit and vegetables before drying. Peaches may be defuzzed with a terry cloth towel or soapless polymer pad (the type used to wash pans). Peel oranges that have dyed skins, but if the skins are natural, leave them on for they are tasty when dried.

If a treatment is desired to prevent discoloration, dip food slices in the solution and drain off excess moisture or pat dry with a towel. Arrange the pieces on a tray, allowing room for air circulation between each slice. Put the tray in the sun, dehydrator, or other warm area to dry. Cover trays with cheesecloth if are not in a dehydrator. Remember to bring in sun-drying trays at night. Sun drying may take several days depending on weather conditions and the type of produce. Dehydrators will dry most food in eight to twenty-four hours. Vegetables will have a moisture content of about 5 percent when ready to store. Fruits, because of their larger sugar content, will retain up to 20 percent moisture. Fruits will feel dry and leathery; vegetables will be crisp. Moist produce will mold quickly. Since organisms need moisture to grow, a very dry product keeps best. To test for moisture, place a sample in a jar after the product has been cooled to room temperature, seal the jar, and leave overnight. Next day check for moisture formation on the side of the jar. If there is any, return the product to the trays for further drying.

Proper storage determines how long dried foods can be kept. Sealed plastic, glass, or metal containers keep out air, bacteria, and bugs. Label and date the containers, for many foods are look-alikes when dried. Put the containers in a cool, dark place. Light will cause oxidation, darkening the product destroying some of the vitamin C and flavor of fruits and vegetables. Air will cause further deterioration.

To reconstitute dried fruits and vegetables, place them in a bowl and cover with lukewarm water. They may take several hours to plump. Fruits can be soaked overnight and be ready for breakfast. Do not throw away any unabsorbed water; it contains nutrients. Drink the excess liquid or use it in a recipe.

Dried sheets of pureed fruit are called "fruit leather" because of their leather-like appearance and texture. The flavor is delicious. To make fruit leathers, blend one or more kinds of fruit until liquid, then spread evenly on a drying tray that has been covered with plastic wrap. For quick drying the layer should be no more than one-quarter-inch thick. When the leather is dry, roll it in sheet of plastic wrap and store in a sealed container if it is not to be used immediately.

Treatments to Prevent Discoloration

Lemon juice. Use one-fouth cup lemon juice to one quart of water. Lemon juice imparts a slight tangy taste to the produce. You may use a little honey with the mixture when dipping fruit, but it will take longer to dry if honey is used.

Ascorbic acid (Vitamin C). Use 3,000 milligrams of ascorbic acid to one quart of water. This dip is satisfactory for most fruits and vegetables. For apples, use 9,000 milligrams of ascorbic acid per cup of water. Peaches, pears, nectarines, and apricots require 4,500 milligrams of ascorbic acid per cup of water.

Salt water. Mix one tablespoon of sea salt to each gallon of water.

Vinegar. Use one tablespoon of vinegar for each gallon of water.

Honey and lemon. Use three cups of honey, four cups of water, and one tablespoon of lemon juice. This is a sweet dip and produces a dessert. Less honey may be used if desired.

HERB TEAS

Herbs are vegetables and, herb teas are beverages made by leaching out some of the vegetable's nutrients into water. Herb teas have been used since prehistoric times for their medicinal qualities and their pleasant taste. The first Chinese herb book dates from about 2700 B.C. and lists 365 medicinal plants and their uses. There are many good books available on the proper use of individual herbs.

As a beverage, herbs make excellent substitutes for caffeine-laden coffee and tea. Cafree, yerba buena, and maté contain no caffeine, yet their flavor is as rich, full-bodied, and satisfying as conventional teas. Instead of coffee try chickory or dandelion root tea. Their flavor is similar to coffee. Mint tea is refreshing, and ginseng is mildly stimulating. There are many varieties of herb teas available. Some you will like immediately while you may have to acquire a taste for others. If you have not tried herb teas, buy a variety package and enjoy a cup of several different kinds. After you become a connoisseur, try making tea with two or more varieties. Possibilities for combination are almost limitless.

The following list is only a sample of the many herbs and spices found in herb shops or health food stores for making teas.

Alfalfa	Fennel	Marshmallow	Sassafras
Anis	Ginger	Mullein	Senna
Blueberry	Ginseng	Nettle	Shavegrass
Burdock	Hibiscus	Oak bark	Slippery elm
Chamomile	Horehound	Oat straw	Spearmint
Catnip	Huckleberry	Papaya leaf	Strawberry leaf
Celery seed	Juniper berries	Parsley	Thyme
Chicory	Knot grass	Peppermint	Watercress
Comfrey root	Lemon grass	Plantain	Yarrow
Cornsilk	Licorice root	Rose hips	Yellow dock
Dandelion	Linden	Sage-cypress	Yerba mate
Fenugreek	Marjoram	Sarsaparilla	Yerba buena

Sun and Vacuum Bottle Teas

Conventional teas are made by steeping herbs in boiling water. Boiling water may cause some destruction or change in certain properties of herbs. It is not necessary to use boiling water to prepare full-bodied tea. Fragrant, flavorful, and healthful raw teas can be made by placing herbs and spices in a glass container of water and setting it in a warm protected spot in the sun. Use one teaspoon of herbs or spices per cup of water, or as recommended on the package. The sun will keep the water warm enough to steep the herbs without cooking them. In three or four hours there will be a full-bodied beverage that is delicious warm or iced. During the winter place the tea jar on a sunny window sill or by a heater duct, or just leave it on the kitchen counter overnight to make breakfast tea.

Making tea in a vacuum bottle is one of the easiest ways to prepare uncooked tea in the winter or summer. Use warm water, about 49° C. (120° F.), and one teaspoon of herbs per cup of water. Put the herbs and water in a vacuum bottle that has been preheated with a rinsing of hot water. Secure the lid and let stand at least two hours, or leave overnight to be ready in the morning. Herb teas can be drunk plain or with honey or lemon.

SPECIAL FOODS

Agar. Agar can make delicious jelled desserts that are 99-percent raw, and is especially useful in making pies, puddings, jelly, ice cream, and aspic. Prepared agar is not a raw food, but since it is capable of taking up to two hundred times its volume in water, very little is needed to make a jell.

Unlike gelatin, agar is of plant origin. It is made from a seaweed. Agar is marketed in several ways, in sticks or blocks, in a mass like fine hair, in powder, or in flakes. It is almost completely tasteless. Though not always available powdered or granular agar is the easiest to use because it dissolves more readily than other types of agar. Flakes are usually easy to find. If flakes are used, more is required by volume because it is less concentrated than in powder or granules. Follow the directions on the package. Agar will jell quickly without refrigeration, so you must work fast once it begins to cool after being dissolved over heat.

Carob (St. John's-Bread). Carob flour is made from the large brown pods of the female carob tree (*Cevatonia siliqua*). The pods contain about 40 percent sugar and 6 percent protein. The flour has a flavor similar to chocolate and may be used as a substitute for chocolate. Powder made from the pods is often sold toasted and looks like dark cocoa. For a raw vegetarian diet, buy the untoasted carob flour, which is lighter in color and has a speckled appearance. Carob not only tastes good, it also contains many vitamins and minerals. Besides sugar and protein, carob contains calcium, phosphorus, iron, potassium, magnesium, silicon, vitamin B-1, vitamin B-2, niacin, and small amounts of vitamin A.

Coconut. Buy only dried coconut that has been prepared without sugar, and comes shredded or in flakes. Recipes in this book call for dried coconut unless fresh is specified. Fresh coconut may be substituted, using a little less water than called for in the recipe.

Pollen. Pollen is the male seed (sperm) of flowers which is spread by the wind or bees and fertilizes kindred plants. One grain of this fine dust is visible only under a microscope. Hand-gathered pollen is sold in powdered form. Bees harvest it in small pellets the size of a pin head. The pellets can be pulverized in a nut mill or used as they are. Pollen comes in a wide range of colors or color combinations: cream, yellow, orange, browns, tans, greenish, purple and even black. Pollen may have a delightful sweet, flower-like flavor or it may taste slightly bitter. The color and flavor of pollen depend on the kind of flower from which it came. Some people like pollen immediately while others must acquire a taste for it.

Pollen averages about 22 percent of amino-acid-balanced protein. Thirty-five grams or one tablespoon, of pollen daily would satisfy an individual's amino acid requirements. This excellent food also contains vitamin A, B, C, D, E and many minerals such as iron, potassium, sodium, magnesium, and calcium. Pollen is usually sold by the ounce and is expensive. Buy your favorite pollen by the pound it keeps well and will cost less.

Tahini. Tahini is ground sesame seed. It is delicious used in vegetable and fruit dishes. Make excellent, creamy salad dressings by replacing oil with tahini. Sweeten tahini with a little honey for a topping or dessert. Tahini is sold in health food stores and specialty stores. Usually the seeds are toasted before they are made into tahini. Raw tahini is available — read the label carefully. You can make your own tahini from sesame seed by grinding the seed very fine in a nut mill. Make it as needed and the tahini will always be fresh.

Sesame seeds are rich in calcium; 100 grams of seeds contain 1,125 milligrams of calcium, or twice that in two glasses of cows' milk. The seeds are 18 percent protein and are a well-balanced source of essential amino acids and small amounts of vitamin E.

HELPFUL KITCHEN EQUIPMENT

A few well-chosen pieces of special equipment will save you time and energy in preparing raw foods. Good equipment is well worth the investment. Electric grinders, juicers, and blenders use very little electricity compared to heating equipment.

Blenders. Blenders are probably the most versatile of all kitchen appliances. They can be used for blending, mincing, grating, chopping, liquifying, and grinding. Efficiency will depend on the make of the blender. When purchasing a blender, investigate many brands and select the one that fits your needs best. See your library for consumer comparison information.

Nut Mills. The nut mill (or coffee grinder) is an inexpensive, electrical machine that is ideal for grinding small seeds, nuts, and small amounts of grains. Nut mills are also useful in grinding dried vegetables and herbs. The mill may be used for chopping parsley fine, as long as no water clings to the leaves after rinsing. Mills take the work out of making nut patties, sauces, and soups.

Hand Grinders. An old-fashioned hand grinder is perfect for grinding sprouted grains and legumes. Run them through twice if you want a very fine grind. Grinders are also useful for nuts and large seeds. Fresh vegetables are best grated or chopped since grinding tends to pulverize them and separate the juices from the pulp.

Juicers. Good juicers are fairly expensive, but are well worth the price if you enjoy fresh raw fruit and vegetable juices and will give many years of service. The centrifugal is better than the expeller type for average home use. Expeller juicers are used in juice bars where many gallons of juice are made daily. The centrifugal juicer extracts more juice from the pulp than the expeller, though the pulp must be removed by hand after every pint (or quart depending on the machine capacity) of juice. The quart capacity juicer may be more practical for a large family or for one who drinks a large amount of juice. It makes enough for immediate use and the basket need not be emptied until you are finished. Centrifugal juicers can be cleaned quickly and easily, especially if a filter is used in the pulp basket.

Graters. One should buy only hand graters made of stainless steel because they will last a lifetime, while plated steel rusts very easily. Graters are available in a variety of blade sizes, and they are invaluable in the kitchen.

Sieves. Sieves are very handy for making thick, juicy, raw dressings and sauces by separating seeds and skin from the pulp and juice. Unlike blenders, a sieve does not mix air into the sauce, which can change the flavor and the texture of food. Like graters, the best sieves are made of stainless steel.

Food Processors. A newcomer to the world of kitchen equipment is the food processor, which operates on the principle of centrifugal force and combines many of the attributes of a mixer, blender, and grinder. The food processor will slice, chop, grind, whip, mix, knead, shred, and make julienne or french cuts. It will not liquefy, but will pulverize certain foods and is a good emulsifier. A food processor will not grind cereal grains, but will grind rolled grains. It will make nut butters, sauces, and bread doughs and will even chop ice. The food processor is versatile, fast, and efficient.

The food processor is also simple to operate. For different tasks one only has to change the blade, which lifts out with nothing to tighten. There are only four basic, easy-to-clean parts: the basket, blade, lid, and plunger. Several different blades are available to give the processor its versatility.

Compared to most small kitchen appliances, the food processor is expensive. But compared to ovens, cooktops, and microwave ovens, the food processor is inexpensive. It is a joy to use and will save many hours in food preparation.

RECIPES

ABOUT THE RECIPES

T he recipes in this book are designed to help satisfy the tastes of those who are accustomed to eating cooked food. When beginning a raw food diet, one may enjoy a few foods with textures similar to the foods one is in the habit of eating. A raw food purist would simply wash food, cut it into manageable pieces, and arrange it attractively on a plate. Salt is not included in any of the recipes. If in the beginning the food seems bland, add a little sea salt, using less and less until salt is eliminated from the diet. Once salt is eliminated subtle flavors never noticed before will emerge. All recipes call for raw food, except those containing agar and cold-pressed oil.

Don't limit yourself to the recipes in the book. It is possible to convert many favorite recipes using cooked foods to raw food. Suggested garnishes are, of course, optional. Ingredients that are followed by an *asterisk* are given in recipes section of this book. Vegetable powder is occasionally called for; it may be found in specialty shops and health food stores.

·SOUPS·

GAZPACHO

¼ cup olive oil
1 small clove garlic, minced
1 cup tomato juice
2 T lemon juice
3 ripe tomatoes, finely chopped
¼ cup finely chopped onion
¼ cup finely chopped green pepper
¼ cup finely chopped red bell pepper
Garnish: Garlic Chips*

Put olive oil, garlic, tomato juice and lemon juice into a blender and blend ten seconds. In a bowl, combine chopped tomatoes, onion, green and red pepper. Pour the tomato mixture over the vegetables and mix well. Serves 2 generously.

ALMOND SOUP

1 cup almonds
2 cups warm water
2 T chopped bell pepper
1 t minced onion
1 T minced parsley
2 T olive oil
Garnish: ¼ cup Parsley Noodles,* crumbled

Rinse almonds and put into a small bowl with the warm water. Soak three or four hours or overnight. Remove the almonds, retaining the water, and slip off skins. Put the almonds, bell pepper, onion, parsley, and oil into a blender, add the retained water, and blend until smooth. Makes about 3 servings.

GREEN PEA SOUP

1 small avocado, peeled and chopped
1 cup green peas
1 T minced green onion
2 sprigs parsley or sweet basil
1 T lemon juice or 4 cherry tomatoes

Whirl all ingredients in a blender until smooth and creamy. If soup is too thick, thin with a little water. Serves 2.

CREAM OF TOMATO SOUP

4 ripe tomatoes
¾ cup warm water
1 T minced onion
½ cup cashews, ground
½ t vegetable powder
Garnish: Croutons* or chopped herbs

Sieve the tomatoes. In a bowl, combine sieved tomatoes, water, onion, cashews, and vegetable powder. Whip mixture with a fork until smooth. Serves 2 to 3.

SPINACH SOUP

¼ cup oatmeal
2 cups warm water
1 bunch young spinach
1 T chopped green onions
1 T chopped mint leaves
Garnish: Dash nutmeg

Soak the oatmeal in the warm water for one hour. Wash the spinach and retain only the leaves. Put the soaked oatmeal, spinach, green onions, and mint leaves into a blender and blend until smooth and creamy. Serves 3.

GREEN LIMA SOUP

1 cup lima beans, fresh or frozen
1 cup warm water
2 T minced parsley
2 T minced celery leaves
1 T chopped onion
Garnish: Chopped parsley or Horseradish Cream*

If frozen lima beans are used, defrost them completely. Whirl all ingredients in a blender until mixture is smooth. Serves 2.

CORN SOUP

2 tender ears of corn
1½ cups warm water
1 t minced onion
1 T oil
1 T chopped red or green pepper
Garnish: Sprig of watercress or parsley

Wash corn and cut the kernels off the cob. Scrape the cob with the edge of a knife to remove the corn germ and remaining juice. Put the cut corn with its juice, water, onion, and oil into a blender. Blend until creamy. Add the pepper and blend about five seconds more. Serves 2.

VEGETABLE SOUP

1 t vegetable broth powder
½ cup water
2 tomatoes, sieved
1 carrot, coarsely grated
¼ cup peas
¼ cup finely chopped celery
1 T finely chopped parsley
1 green onion, finely chopped

Dissolve the vegetable broth in the water, put all ingredients into a bowl, and mix well. Add more water if soup is too thick. Serves 2.

BROCCOLI SOUP

1 cup chopped broccoli
1 cup warm water
2 T finely ground sunflower seed
Garnish: Chopped parsley

Blend broccoli, water, and ground sunflower seed together for about thirty seconds. Serves 2.
VARIATION: Use potato juice instead of water. Use tahini or almond butter in place of sunflower seed.

WATERCRESS SOUP

1 bunch watercress
3 cups warm water
1 T minced onion
3 T tahini or cashew butter
Garnish: Croutons* or chopped watercress

Wash watercress, discarding tough stalks. Put the leaves into a blender with warm water, onion, and nut butter. Blend until smooth and creamy. Serves 3.

·ENTREES·

NOODLE-STUFFED PEPPERS

1½ cups crumbled Parsley Noodles*
½   t vegetable powder
¼   t sweet basil
¼   cup warm water
2   red or green bell peppers
¼   cup coarsely chopped walnuts
2   T minced onion
4   mushrooms, finely chopped

Sauce: 2 T Tahini Mayonnaise* or Sesame Tomato Sauce*

Put the noodles into a mixing bowl. Mix together the vegetable powder, basil, and warm water, and pour over the noodles. Cut the tops off the peppers and scoop out the seeds and pith. Add walnuts, onion, and mushrooms to the noodles and mix well. Spoon the mixture into the peppers and garnish if desired. Serves 2.

SPROUTED GRAIN BURGERS

½   cup oatmeal
¼   cup water
1   cup wheat sprouts, coarsely ground
1   cup lentil sprouts, coarsely ground
¼   cup chopped green pepper
1   tomato, finely chopped
2   T minced green onion
½   small clove garlic, minced
1   stalk celery, chopped
2   T minced parsley
¼   t cumin
½   t chili powder
¼   t dry mustard

Sauce: Sesame Tomato Sauce* or Mexican Hot Sauce*

Soak the oatmeal in water for fifteen minutes. Then combine all the ingredients, mix thoroughly, and shape into patties. Makes 2 to 3 servings.

VARIATION: Use either rye sprouts or triticale sprouts instead of wheat sprouts.

HAZELNUT CAKES

```
1   cup hazelnuts, ground
¼   cup cornmeal
2   T oil
    water
```

In a bowl, combine nuts, cornmeal, and oil, adding enough water to make a thick mixture. Shape mixture into little cakes. Makes 3 servings.

SUCCOTASH

```
    pinch of basil and rosemary
1   t lemon juice
1   t oil
2   t water
½   cup peas
½   cup corn
½   cup lima beans
¼   cup red or green pepper
1   T chopped chives
    chopped almonds
```

In a cup, combine the herbs, lemon juice, oil, and water; set aside for ten minutes. Combine the peas, corn, lima beans, pepper, and chives. Pour the herb dressing over the vegetables; toss lightly. Sprinkle chopped almonds over the vegetables. Serves 2.

GUACAMOLE TOSTADAS

```
½   cup peanuts, ground
½   cup Brazil nuts, ground
1-3 t chili powder
    water
1   small avocado
1   T lemon juice
½   t dried cilantro or
    1 T minced fresh cilantro
4   seven-inch Cornmeal Tostada Shells*
¼   cup finely chopped onions
2   cups shredded lettuce
1   tomato, finely chopped
```
Sauce: Mexican Hot Sauce*

Combine ground nuts, chili powder, and enough water to make a creamy paste, about the consistency of thick white sauce. Peel and pit the avocado. Put the avocado, lemon juice, and cilantro into a bowl and whip until smooth and creamy. Spread a thick layer of nut paste over a Cornmeal Tostada Shell, sprinkle with onions, and cover with a thick layer of shredded lettuce. Cover the lettuce with a layer of avocado mixture and top with the chopped tomatoes. Repeat procedure with remaining tostada shells. Serves 2 generously.

VARIATIONS: Use any kind of nuts desired. Instead of cornmeal shells use wheat or millet. Instead of making guacamole, use sliced avocado and omit the lemon juice and the cilantro. Use alfalfa sprouts instead of lettuce.

LIMA BEAN LOAF

1½ cups fresh or frozen lima beans, ground
¼ cup chopped onion
¼ cup chopped celery
2 T oil
½ cup finely chopped parsley
½ small clove garlic
½ t thyme

Sauce: Tomato-Herb Dressing*, Sesame Tomato Sauce*, Mexican Hot Sauce*, or Avocado Dressing*

Put all ingredients, except the dressing, into a mixing bowl, mix thoroughly, and shape into a loaf. To serve, cut the loaf into thick slices. Serves 2 to 3.

CARROT-NUT PATTIES

2 cups grated carrots
¼ cup sesame seed, ground
¼ cup sunflower seed, ground
2 T finely chopped onion
2 T finely chopped celery
½ t fine herbs

Sauce: Sesame Tomato Sauce*

Combine all ingredients and mix well. Shape mixture into patties or walnut-sized balls. Makes 2 to 3 servings.

SUNFLOWER SEED CAKES

1 cup sunflower seed, coarsely ground
¼ cup rice polish
1 T chopped onion
water

Sauce: Mexican Hot Sauce*

Combine ground seeds, rice polish, and chopped onion, and add enough water to make a thick mixture. Shape into little cakes. This is delicious served plain or with Mexican Hot Sauce. Makes 2 to 3 servings.

VEGETABLE CURRY

1 zucchini, thinly sliced
2 mushrooms, thinly sliced
1 carrot, thinly sliced
¼ cup chopped green pepper
1 T chopped onion
1 cup lentil sprouts
¼ t chili powder
1 t curry powder
2 T ground sunflower seed
¼ cup water
1 t kelp granules

Put vegetables and sprouts into a mixing bowl. In a cup, combine chili powder, curry powder, sunflower seed, kelp, and water. Whip mixture with a fork until smooth. Pour over the vegetables and mix well. Serves 2.

MOCK TURKEY LOAF

¼ cup Brazil nuts, ground
½ cup pumpkin or squash seed, ground
½ cup cashews, ground
½ t sage
1 T minced onion
1½ cups finely chopped celery
1 T minced parsley
Sauce: Cranberry Relish*

Combine all ingredients except relish and mix well. Shape mixture into a loaf. Serve in thick slices with a spoonful of Cranberry Relish on the side. Makes 2 or 3 servings.

MUSHROOM PATTIES

2 cups chopped mushrooms
1 T oil
¼ cup chopped onion
¼ cup chopped green pepper
1 cup wheat germ or oatmeal
¼ t marjoram
  pinch rosemary
Sauce: Sesame Tomato Sauce*

Combine all ingredients except sauce and mix well. Form mixture into a loaf, patties, or small balls. Makes 2 or 3 servings.

BEAN SPROUT BURGERS

2 cups bean sprouts, chopped
¼ cup ground sunflower seed
¼ cup coarsely chopped pecans
1 T finely chopped onion
1 T finely chopped parsley
¼ t kelp granules
Sauce: Tomato-Herb Dressing*

Combine all ingredients and form into patties. Top with dressing. Serves 2.

LENTIL-SPROUT BALLS

2 cups lentil sprouts, coarsely ground
¼ cup nut butter
¼ cup finely chopped celery
2 T finely chopped green onion
1 small carrot, grated
¼ sweet basil
Sauce: Sesame Tomato Sauce*

Combine all ingredients and mix well. Form mixture into one-inch balls and serve plain or over spaghetti squash with Sesame Tomato Sauce. Serves 2.

LOOKS-LIKE PIZZA

4 Tostada Shells*
   olive oil
½ cup Tomato-Herb Dressing*
½ cup chopped green peppers
½ small red onion, thinly sliced
2 mushrooms, thinly sliced
1 Sunflower Seed-Nut Roll*
2 T chopped parsley
½ cup alfalfa sprouts

Brush each tostada shell with olive oil and spread with Tomato-Herb Dressing. Add a layer of green pepper, onion, and mushroom. Arrange the nut roll slices over the vegetables. Top with parsley and sprouts. Makes four seven-inch pizzas.

YAM LOAF

1 cup grated yams
½ cup Brazil nuts, ground
¼ cup ground oatmeal
2 T sesame seed
2 T chopped onion
¼ cup chopped celery
¼ cup chopped mushrooms
¼ cup chopped green pepper

Combine all ingredients and mix thoroughly. Shape mixture into a loaf. Makes 2 to 3 servings.

CRUNCHY WALNUT LOAF

1 cup grated carrots
¼ cup finely chopped onion
½ cup finely chopped celery
¼ cup coarsely ground sunflower seed
¼ cup coarsely chopped walnuts
2 T oil
½ cup oatmeal

In a bowl, combine all ingredients and mix well. Shape into a loaf and serve in slices. Serves 2.

SUNFLOWER SEED-NUT ROLL

¼ cup Brazil nuts, ground
½ cup sunflower seed, ground
¼ cup sesame seed, ground
2 T minced onion
1 t kelp granules
1 t chili powder (optional)
   water

Combine nuts, seeds, onion, kelp, and chili powder. Mix well and add enough water to make a stiff dough. Roll dough into a one-inch log. To serve, cut into slices. If not used immediately, wrap in wax paper and store in the refrigerator. Serves 2.

·VEGETABLES·

CAULIFLOWER VERDE

½ head cauliflower
6 T Lemon Dressing*
1 large avocado
2 T minced onion
¼ cup coarsely ground almonds
   dash nutmeg
   salad greens
1 tomato, cut into wedges, ¼ cup
   sliced radishes

Break the cauliflower into small pieces, put into a bowl, and pour over half of the Lemon Dressing. Marinate 30 minutes. Peel and mash avocado and mix with marinade drained from the cauliflower and the remaining dressing. Add onion, almonds, and nutmeg and whip until creamy. Cover individual salad plates with a bed of greens and arrange the cauliflower over the greens. Pour the avocado sauce over and top with tomato wedges and radishes. Makes 2 generous servings.

PERSIAN CUCUMBERS

¾ cup Tahini Mayonnaise
   water
¼ cup minced onion
½ t dried mint
¼ t dried marjoram or basil
2 cucumbers, coarsely grated
4 lettuce leaves
Garnish: 2 T raisins, plumped with water, ¼ cup chopped walnuts

Thin Tahini Mayonnaise with enough water to obtain the consistency of heavy cream. Add onion, mint, and marjoram and mix thoroughly. Pour the dressing over the grated cucumbers and toss lightly. Place the lettuce leaves on salad plates. Put the cucumber mixture on the lettuce and garnish with the raisins and walnuts. Makes 4 servings.

MUSHROOMS AND BEAN SPROUTS

½ lb mushrooms, thinly sliced
2 cups bean sprouts
2 T chopped chives
½ head cabbage, shredded
½ cup Ginger-Soy Sauce*

Combine mushrooms, bean sprouts, and chives. Put the cabbage on a platter and cover with vegetables. Pour sauce over just before serving. Makes 3 or 4 servings.

STUFFED TOMATOES

4 tomatoes
½ cup Tahini Mayonnaise*
1 cup diced celery
2 T minced chives or green onions
2 T minced fresh dill or ½ t dried dill
   salad greens

Cut off the tops of the tomatoes and scoop out the pulp and seeds. Chop the pulp; drain off two tablespoons of juice to be mixed with the Tahini Mayonnaise. To the tomato pulp, add celery, chives, and dill. Mix well, add half of the mayonnaise-juice mixture, and blend. Fill tomato shells with the mixture and serve on salad greens. Garnish with the remaining mayonnaise. Makes 4 servings.

CURRIED CUCUMBERS

2 T oil
1 T lemon juice
1 t honey
1 t curry powder
1 T soy sauce
1 small clove garlic, minced
2 cucumbers, chopped

Combine all ingredients except cucumbers and whip with a fork until thoroughly mixed. Pour dressing over cucumbers and toss lightly. Makes 4 servings.

GARDEN SALAD

1 head butter or Boston lettuce, broken
1 carrot, diced
1 cup shredded red cabbage
1 cup green peas
2 green onions, chopped
1 tomato, chopped
1 zucchini or cucumber, sliced paper-thin
1 cup alfalfa sprouts
   French*, Lemon*, or Italian Dressing*

Combine all ingredients and toss lightly with dressing. Makes 4 servings.

GINGER TURNIPS AND CARROTS

   salad greens
2 carrots, thinly sliced
2 turnips, thinly sliced
1 T vinegar
2 t honey
1 T lemon juice
1 T water
¼ t grated fresh ginger

Arrange salad greens on salad plates, then cover with the carrots and turnips. Mix together vinegar, honey, lemon juice, water, and ginger in a small bowl, pour dressing over vegetables, and serve at once. Makes 2 to 3 servings.

ONION MINT SALAD

1 red onion, thinly sliced
1 cup fresh, whole mint leaves
2 T lemon juice
3 T oil
Garnish: Whole-wheat Vegetable Crackers* or Tostadas*

Combine onion, mint, lemon, and oil and toss lightly. Serve with Whole-wheat Vegetable Crackers* or Tostadas* broken into cracker-size pieces. Makes 2 servings.

CAULIFLOWER-HERB SALAD

   salad greens
1 tomato, sliced
½ head cauliflower
½ cup Tahini Mayonnaise*
1 T lemon juice
1 T minced parsley
1 T minced chives
¼ cup chopped red or green bell pepper

Place the greens on individual salad plates and cover with the sliced tomatoes. Break the cauliflower into small pieces and arrange over the tomatoes. Mix Tahini Mayonnaise with lemon juice, parsley, and chives, pour evenly over the salad, then sprinkle each salad with red or green peppers. Makes 2 large servings.

CABBAGE AND BEET SALAD

1 head cabbage, finely chopped
2 beets, finely chopped
1 small green or red bell pepper, finely chopped
1 cup Tahini Mayonnaise*
2 T vinegar or lemon juice
1 T honey

Mix cabbage, beets, and pepper. Thin Tahini Mayonnaise with vinegar or lemon juice and add the honey. Pour dressing over salad and mix thoroughly. Makes 4 servings.

60

GREEN BEAN SALAD

½ lb green beans
1 cup mung bean sprouts
1 cucumber, diced
3 T lemon juice
1 t honey
   dash garlic powder
   oregano to taste

Stem and cut beans into one-inch-long julienne pieces. Put together beans, mung sprouts, and cucumbers in a salad bowl. Whip together lemon juice, honey, garlic powder and oregano in a cup with a fork until well blended, then pour over the salad. Toss until vegetables are coated. Serves 3 to 4.

MARINATED ZUCCHINI SLICES

4 small zucchini, thinly sliced
1 lemon, juice of
½ clove garlic, crushed
3 T olive oil
   grind of pepper

Put zucchini into a bowl, add remaining ingredients, and mix well. Refrigerate to chill and marinate for at least one-half hour. Makes 3 to 4 servings.

MARINATED ASPARAGUS

1 lb asparagus
1 T soy sauce
1 T sesame oil
½ t honey
   salad greens

Snap off and discard tough ends of asparagus and chop stalks into half-inch pieces. Combine soy sauce, oil, and honey. Pour marinade over the asparagus. Mix well and serve on a bed of greens. Makes 2 to 3 servings.

WATERCRESS SALAD

1 T lemon juice
3 T safflower oil
1 T honey
½ t fresh, grated horseradish
1 bunch watercress, stemmed
1 head Boston or butter lettuce
½ cup Sprouted Grain Chips*

In a small bowl, combine lemon juice, oil, and honey, beat until smooth, add horseradish, and beat again. Break watercress and lettuce into bite-size pieces. Pour dressing over the greens and toss lightly. Add chips and toss only until evenly mixed. Makes 4 servings.

ROMAINE SPROUT BOATS

2 cups alfalfa sprouts
2 T finely chopped red onion
¼ cup French Dressing*
4 medium-size romaine leaves
½ cup sprouted sunflower seed

Combine alfalfa sprouts, onion, and salad dressing. Divide salad into four parts and fill the cavities of romaine leaves. Sprinkle sunflower seed sprouts over the alfalfa sprouts. Serves 2 as sandwiches, eaten out of the hand, or makes 4 small salads.

BRAZIL NUT-SPINACH SALAD

1 lb baby leaf spinach, stemmed
¼ cup water
2 T lemon juice
¼ t dry mustard
¼ cup Brazil nuts, ground
1 t honey
  grind of pepper
4 radishes, thinly sliced

Tear spinach into bite-size pieces. In a small bowl, combine water, lemon juice, mustard, Brazil nuts, honey, and pepper. Whip until smooth and creamy. Pour the dressing over spinach and radishes and toss until leaves are coated. Makes 2 to 3 servings.

STUFFED AVOCADO HALVES

2 T oil
1 T lemon juice
¼ t paprika
1 tomato, finely chopped
1 green onion, finely chopped
½ clove garlic, minced
1 large avocado

In a bowl, combine oil, lemon juice, and paprika. Whip dressing with a fork until creamy; add tomato, onion, and garlic. Mix well. Cut avocado in half lengthwise and remove the pit. Fill the avocado centers with tomato mixture. Makes 2 servings.

SWEET POTATO SALAD

1 t honey
¼ cup orange juice
  dash nutmeg
  dash cinnamon
1 cup grated sweet potato
2 T raisins
¼ cup chopped nuts

Mix honey, orange juice, nutmeg, and cinnamon. Combine the sweet potato, raisins, and nuts. Pour honey mixture over the salad and toss lightly. Makes 2 servings.

COLORFUL CUCUMBER SALAD

1 cucumber, thinly sliced
½ cup coarsely grated carrot
6 radishes, thinly sliced
¼ cup tahini
1 t chopped mint
2 t honey
3 T water
2 T lemon juice
watercress or salad greens

Put the cucumber slices, carrot, and radish slices into a salad bowl. Combine tahini, mint, honey, water, and lemon juice, whip with a fork until creamy, pour over the salad, and toss lightly. Serve on a bed of watercress or salad greens. Serves 2.

GYPSY BEETS

1 cup coarsely grated beets
½ cup coarsely grated carrots
½ cup finely chopped beet greens
2 t honey
1 T lemon juice
2 large lettuce leaves

In a large bowl, combine beets, carrots, and greens. Dissolve honey in the lemon juice and pour over the salad. Put the lettuce leaves on individual salad plates. Toss the salad lightly and fill the leaves with the mixture. Serves 2.

GREEN PEA SALAD

2 cups green peas
2 T oil
2 T lemon juice
2 T minced chives
½ cup minced green pepper
salad greens

Combine all ingredients except salad greens and toss lightly. Serve on individual salad plates of greens. Serves 2 or 3.

CRUNCHY GARDEN SALAD

1 small head butter or leaf lettuce
1 carrot, thinly sliced
¼ head red cabbage, shredded
1 cup raw peas
2 green onions, chopped
½ cup cauliflower, broken into small pieces
1 tomato, cut into thin wedges
1 zucchini, thinly sliced
½ cup alfalfa sprouts
dressing

Break the lettuce into bite-size pieces. Put all ingredients into a salad bowl. Toss with your favorite salad dressing. Makes 3 to 4 servings.

KING COLE SLAW

    1 cup shredded red cabbage
    1 cup shredded green cabbage
    ½ cup grated carrots
    ¼ cup raisins
       dash cayenne pepper
    1 T caraway seed
    ½ t celery seed
    2 T lemon juice
    ¼ t dry mustard
    2 t honey
    ¼ cup ground sesame seed
    ¼ cup ground sunflower seed
    2 whole cabbage leaves
       dill seed

In a mixing bowl, combine red and green cabbage, carrots, raisins, cayenne pepper, caraway seed, and celery seed. In a small bowl or blender, mix lemon juice, dry mustard, honey, sesame, and sunflower seeds until smooth and creamy. Pour this mixture over the cabbage mixture and toss until well mixed. Place whole cabbage leaves on salad plates, and fill the leaves with slaw. Sprinkle with dill seed. Makes 2 to 3 servings.

SPINACH AND MUSHROOM SALAD

    1 lb spinach
    3 T chopped chives
    2 white or red radishes, thinly sliced
   10 small mushrooms, sliced
    1 carrot, cut in one-inch strips
       French Dressing*

Tear spinach into bite-size pieces, add other ingredients, and toss lightly with French Dressing. Makes 2 to 3 servings.

SUMMER SALAD

    1 head leaf lettuce
    1 zucchini, sliced
    1 turnip, thinly sliced
    1 cup cauliflower flowerets
    2 stalks celery, chopped
    2 green onions, chopped
    2 carrots, cut into strips
    6 cherry tomatoes or 1 tomato, cut
       into wedges
    1 green pepper sliced
    1 bunch watercress
    1 cup alfalfa sprouts
    ½ cup dressing, oil, or cream

Line salad bowl with leaf lettuce. Prepare all the vegetables. Put the vegetables in the lettuce-lined bowl and pour the dressing evenly over the salad. Makes 2 large servings.

FOUR BEAN SALAD

1 cup chopped green beans
1 cup chopped wax beans
1 cup fresh or frozen lima beans
1 cup bean sprouts
1 green onion, chopped
½ clove garlic, minced
¼ cup dressing: Herb*, Chervil*, or French*
   salad greens

Combine beans, sprouts, onion, and garlic. Add dressing and toss lightly. Serve on a bed of greens. Makes 2 to 3 servings.

CELERY ROOT

1 lb celery root
½ cup French Dressing*
   salad greens

Scrub celery root, peel it, and slice into julienne strips. Put strips into a small bowl and pour French Dressing over. Toss lightly and let marinate for a couple of hours. Serve on a bed of greens. Serves 3.

AVOCADO SALAD

2 avocados, chopped
1 T lemon juice
1 t cilantro leaves, crumbled
2 tomatoes, chopped
¼ t chili powder
2 T olive oil
1 T minced onion
   dash cayenne
   salad greens

Combine avocado, lemon juice, cilantro, and tomatoes and set aside. In a cup, combine chili powder, olive oil, onion, and cayenne. Whip dressing with a fork until creamy. Pour dressing over avocado salad and toss lightly. Serve on a bed of greens. Makes 4 servings.

ROMAINE SALAD

1 head romaine lettuce
1 small bunch leaf lettuce
1 tomato, cut in wedges
1 cucumber, sliced
2 green onions, chopped
½ avocado, peeled and sliced
¼ cup French* or Lemon Dressing*
¼ t tarragon, crumbled

Tear lettuce into bite-size pieces, add tomatoes, cucumbers, onions, and avocados. Toss with dressing and tarragon. Makes 4 servings.

ASSYRIAN SALAD

1 cup wheat sprouts
3 tomatoes, finely chopped
½ cucumber, finely chopped
2 green onions, finely chopped
2 T olive oil
½ lemon, juice of
½ avocado, sliced lengthwise

Combine all ingredients except the avocado and mix well. Serve in individual salad bowls. Top with avocado slices. Makes 2 generous servings.

LEEK SALAD

2 young tender leeks
2 tomatoes, chopped
½ t dry basil or 1 T fresh basil
¼ cup French Dressing*
leaf lettuce
Garnish: ¼ cup Croutons*

Cut leeks into pieces about ½-inch long. Mix leeks, tomatoes, and basil, add dressing, and toss lightly. Cover two salad plates with lettuce leaves. Spoon the salad over the leaves and garnish with Croutons. Makes 2 servings.

GINGER CUCUMBERS

2 small cucumbers, sliced paper-thin
½ lemon, juice of
2 T water
2 t finely chopped fresh dill weed or ¼ t dried dill weed
1 t shredded fresh ginger

Put cucumbers in a bowl. Combine remaining ingredients and pour over the cucumbers. Chill before serving. Makes 2 servings.

CUCUMBERS IN CREAM

2 small cucumbers, chopped
2 radishes, chopped
1 T minced parsley
2 T finely chopped onion
1 T minced dill
¼ cup Tahini Mayonnaise*
¼ cup unsweetened Coconut Cream*
1 T vinegar
½ clove garlic, minced
2 large lettuce leaves

Combine cucumbers, radishes, parsley, onions, and dill in a salad bowl. In a small bowl, combine Tahini Mayonnaise, Coconut Cream, vinegar, and garlic. Whip with a fork until well blended. Pour dressing over vegetables and toss lightly until mixed. Put the lettuce leaves on individual salad plates and fill them with the salad. Makes 2 servings.

·DRESSINGS & SPREADS·

FRENCH DRESSING

- ¼ cup lemon juice
- 2 T water
- 2 t honey
- ¼ t dry mustard
  dash cayenne
- ½ cup oil

Put all ingredients into a blender and liquefy for 30 seconds. Makes about ¾ cup.

GARLIC DRESSING

- 2 cloves garlic, crushed
- ¼ cup lemon juice
- ¼ cup safflower oil
- 2 T minced parsley
- 1 t dill weed

Liquefy all ingredients in a blender for 15 seconds. Makes ½ cup.

HORSERADISH CREAM

- ¼ cup tahini or ground sesame seed
- 2 T lemon juice
- 2 t grated horseradish
- 2 T water

Put ingredients in a small mixing bowl and whip with a fork until smooth and creamy. Add more water if necessary, consistency should be like heavy cream. Excellent served over thinly sliced cucumbers and radishes. Makes about ½ cup.

MINT DRESSING

- ½ cup olive oil
- 2 T lemon juice
- 2 T water
- 2 t minced mint leaves

Mix all ingredients and let stand for 30 minutes. Tasty over fruits or vegetables. Makes about ¾ cup.

FRESH BASIL DRESSING

1 cup fresh basil leaves
1 small clove garlic, chopped
1 green onion, chopped
1 small tomato, peeled and seeded
¼ cup ground almonds
6 Brazil nuts, ground
1 lemon, juice of
  water

Put all ingredients into a blender and mix until smooth, adding only enough water to make a thick dressing. Serve over spaghetti squash, sprouts, or green salad. Makes 2 servings (about ¾ cup).

SESAME TOMATO SAUCE

1 cup sieved tomato purée
¼ cup ground sesame seed
1 T minced parsley
1 t minced onion

Combine all ingredients and whip until creamy. Use sauce as a topping for nut, vegetable-nut, and vegetable patties or balls. Makes about 1 cup.
VARIATIONS: Add 1 t curry powder or 2 t chili powder or 1½ t fines herbes.

ITALIAN DRESSING

2 T chopped onion
1 small clove garlic
1 t honey
2 T red wine vinegar
½ cup olive oil
1 small ripe tomato
¼ t dry mustard
¼ t oregano leaves
  dash paprika

Put all ingredients into a blender and liquefy for 30 seconds. Delicious served over leafy greens. Makes about 1 cup.

CITRUS PEEL DRESSING

2 T apple cider vinegar
2 T lemon juice
2 t honey
¼ t nutmeg
½ t grated orange peel
½ t grated lemon peel
1 t chervil
½ cup sesame oil

Put all ingredients into a blender and blend until creamy. Compliments fruits or vegetables, especially spinach. Makes ¾ cup.

CHERVIL DRESSING

2 T apple cider vinegar
2 T lemon juice
1 t chervil
¼ t marjoram
¼ t nutmeg
½ t grated lemon peel
1 t grated orange peel
1 T honey
½ cup sesame oil

Put all ingredients into a blender and blend until creamy. This dressing compliments vegetable or fruit salads. Makes about ¾ cup.

ALMOND-GARLIC DRESSING

12 almonds
    water
2 cloves garlic
¼ cup lemon juice
¾ cup olive oil

Cover almonds with water and soak until plump. Remove the skins, put the almonds in a blender, add garlic, and grind the almonds. Turn the blender on again and beat in olive oil in a thin stream. Add lemon juice and whip until creamy. Excellent served over lettuce or greens. Makes 1 cup.

HONEY DRESSING

½ cup honey
¼ t mustard
1 t paprika
½ cup lemon juice
½ cup oil

Put the honey, mustard, paprika, and lemon juice into a blender. Mix well. Add the oil slowly, blending until smooth. Honey dressing is very good on dessert salads and fresh fruits. Makes about 1½ cups.

HERB DRESSING

⅓ cup ground walnuts
2 T tahini or ground sesame seed
⅔ cup water
¼ t minced garlic
   dash of cayenne
¼ t tarragon
¼ t marjoram
⅛ t thyme
¼ t sweet basil
½ t honey

Put all ingredients in a blender and mix for 30 seconds. Makes 1 cup.

LEMON DRESSING

3 T lemon juice
½ cup olive oil
1 t honey
2 T water
1 t kelp granules
½ t grated lemon peel

Combine all ingredients and mix well. Makes about ¾ cup.

PESTO

1 cup chopped walnuts
1 bunch fresh basil
¼ cup olive oil
1 small clove garlic

Put all ingredients into a blender and blend for 30 seconds. This sauce is delicious served over a bed of alfalfa sprouts, bean sprouts, or spaghetti squash. Makes enough for 2 or 3 servings.

ORANGE DRESSING

¼ cup tahini
4 T honey
½ cup orange juice
1 t lemon juice
1 t grated fresh orange peel

Put all ingredients into a mixing bowl and whip until creamy. This dressing is excellent served over fresh fruit and topped with grated coconut. Makes about 1 cup.

COCONUT DRESSING

¼ cup shredded coconut
1 T lemon juice
1 T honey
1 T pollen (optional)
2 T water or orange juice

Blend all ingredients until creamy. Serve with fruit. Makes about ½ cup.

MINT SAUCE

3 T finely chopped mint leaves
¼ cup lemon juice
2 T water
2 T honey

Whirl all ingredients in a blender for 15 seconds. Mint sauce goes well with citrus fruits or root salads. Makes about ½ cup.

DRIED FRUIT SPREAD

6 pitted dates
6 figs
1 T ground cashews
  water
  Sun Bread*

Put dates, figs, and cashews into a blender. Blend, adding enough water to make a creamy spread. Serve with Sun Bread. Makes about ½ cup.

GINGER-SOY SAUCE

2 T soy sauce
2 T lemon juice or vinegar
2 t honey
½ t grated ginger

Combine all ingredients. Makes ½ cup dressing. Good over vegetables.

CARAWAY MAYONNAISE

½ cup Tahini Mayonnaise*
1 T vinegar
1 t grated onion
1 t caraway
1 t honey

Combine all ingredients and whip with a fork until fluffy. Makes about ½ cup.

TAHINI MAYONNAISE

½ cup tahini
¼ cup lemon juice
4-6 T water

Blend the tahini and lemon juice together at medium speed, adding enough water to make a thick mayonnaise. Store in a sealed jar in the refrigerator until needed. The flavor and nutrition are best if mayonnaise is made the day it is to be used. Makes about 1 cup.

AVOCADO DRESSING OR DIP

1 medium avocado, peeled and seeded
1 T lemon juice
½ t cilantro
¼ t chili powder
2 t minced onion
  dash garlic powder
  dash cayenne

Mash avocado with lemon juice until well mixed. Add remaining ingredients and whip until creamy. Serve with green salad, on tostadas, or as a dip. Makes about 1 cup.
VARIATION: Add one small, finely chopped tomato.

PARSLEY SAUCE

½ cup minced parsley
4 T nut butter, walnut or tahini
2 T water
2 T lemon juice
2 T oil

Put all ingredients into a blender and blend until smooth. Serve over noodles, spaghetti squash, sprouts, or nut patties. Makes ½ cup.

PAPAYA SEED DRESSING

½ cup salad oil
¼ cup honey
¼ t dry mustard
¼ cup lemon juice
2 T chopped onion
1 T fresh papaya seed

Put the oil, honey, mustard, and lemon juice into a blender, blend until smooth, then add onion and papaya seed and blend until papaya seed is the size of coarse ground pepper. This dressing has a piquant flavor and is excellent served with fruit or green salads. Makes about 1 cup.

GREEN MAYONNAISE

1 cup Tahini Mayonnaise*
2 t finely chopped chives
1 t tarragon leaves, crumbled
1 T finely chopped parsley
½ t chervil, crumbled
½ t dill weed

Blend all ingredients. Serve over salads or float a spoonful on soups. It is also delicious served as a dip or spread on crackers. Makes about 1 cup.

HERB MAYONNAISE

½ cup Tahini Mayonnaise*
½ clove garlic, minced
2 T minced chives or green onion
1 T minced parsley
1 T minced red or green pepper

Combine all ingredients, mix lightly. Serve over salad greens or vegetables. Makes about ¾ cup.

MEXICAN HOT SAUCE

2 ripe tomatoes, sieved
1 clove garlic, minced
½ t cilantro, minced
1 T minced onion
1 T olive oil
   ground hot chili to taste

Combine all ingredients and refrigerate until needed. This sauce is excellent for topping tostadas. It is also delicious served over nut patties and vegetables. Makes about ¾ cup.

TOMATO-HERB DRESSING

1 cup sieved tomato pulp
2 T ground sunflower seed
½ small clove garlic, minced
¼ t fines herbes or pinch of each: thyme, oregano, sage, rosemary, marjoram, and basil.

Combine all ingredients. Serve over nut patties or vegetables. Makes about 1 cup.

BANANA DRESSING

1 large banana, sliced
1 lemon, juice of
½ t grated lemon peel
1 T honey

Place all ingredients into a blender and blend until smooth. This is a perfect dressing for fruit. Makes about 1 cup.

ORANGE CREAM TOPPING

1 cup dried, shredded coconut
½ cup orange juice
1 t grated orange peel
1 t lemon juice
2 t honey

Grind the coconut into a butter. Put coconut, along with remaining ingredients, into a blender. Blend until smooth and creamy. Serve over fruits. Makes about ¾ cup.

FRESH COCONUT CREAM

1 fresh coconut
  water
  honey
  vanilla

With a paring knife, make a hole in the soft spot at the end of the coconut. Drain the coconut milk into a glass and set aside. Break open the coconut and remove the meat. The brown peel can be removed easily with a potato peeler. Cut the coconut into small pieces. Grind the pieces as finely as possible in a blender, nut mill, or hand grinder. Put the ground coconut with the coconut milk into a blender and blend at high speed until the mixture is as thick as whipped cream. Add enough water to make desired consistency. Add honey and vanilla to taste. Use as you would whipped cream, over fruits and desserts. Makes about 1 cup.
VARIATION: Omit the honey and vanilla. Add your favorite herbs and serve over vegetables or float a spoonful on a bowl of soup. Coconut cream can be made with dried coconut and water. This will produce a sweeter cream.

HONEY BUTTER

1 part honey
1 part nut or seed butter

Mix thoroughly and store in a sealed jar until needed. Serve on breads, crackers, or over fruit. Add a little water or fruit juice and create a delicious sauce.

DATE BUTTER

1 part honey
1 part nut or seed butter
1 part ground dates

Mix until smooth and creamy. Use the same way as Honey Butter.*

·FRUITS·

BREAKFAST OR DESSERT PEARS

2 pears, finely grated
¼ cup cashews, ground

Spoon finely grated pears into two sherbet cups and top each with two tablespoons of ground cashews. Serve at once. Makes 2 servings.

MUESLI

2 T oatmeal, soaked overnight in ⅓ cup water
2 T finely ground almonds
1 T lemon juice
1 T honey
2 apples, grated
¼ cup pine nuts or chopped almonds

In a bowl, combine soaked oatmeal, ground almonds, lemon juice and honey. Whip with a fork until emulsified. Add grated apples and mix well. Spoon into individual bowls and sprinkle with pine nuts or chopped almonds. Serve at once. Makes 2 servings.

WHIPPED RASPBERRIES

2 cups raspberries
¼ cup mild honey

Put raspberries and honey into a blender and whip until smooth. Chill. Makes 2 or 3 servings.

APPLESAUCE

2 apples, cored and chopped
2 t honey
1 t lemon juice
¼ cup apple juice or water
½ t cinnamon
⅛ t nutmeg

Blend all ingredients in a blender until smooth. Makes 2 servings.

SPICED APRICOTS

1 cup dried apricots
1 cup warm water
1 T honey
½ lemon, thinly sliced
1 stick cinnamon
3 whole allspice
Garnish: Coconut Cream*

Wash apricots and put them in a bowl. Add water and remaining ingredients. Soak overnight. Remove lemon and spices. Serve plain or garnish with a spoonful of Coconut Cream. Makes 2 servings.

VARIATION: Remove the lemon and spices. Put the apricots and soaking water into a blender and whip until creamy, adding more water if too thick.

JUNE SALAD

1 cup cherries, pitted and halved
1 cup plums, pitted and quartered
1 banana, sliced
1 cup raspberries

Combine fruit and serve in sherbet dishes. Makes 2 or 3 servings.

FRUIT-FILLED WATERMELON

½ small watermelon, cut lengthwise
1 cup strawberries
3 oranges, in sections
1 cup pineapple cubes
1 lb seedless grapes
1 T lemon juice
Garnish: sprig of mint

Using a melon baller, scoop out balls from the watermelon. Remove seeds from the balls. Combine melon balls with the remaining fruit and sprinkle with the lemon juice. Mix fruit gently and pour it into the watermelon shell. Fill a shot glass with toothpicks and let your guests spear their own fruit. Makes 1 melon boat.

MELON SURPRISE

3 cups melon balls
1 cup raspberries, strawberries or blackberries
2 T orange juice

Combine all ingredients and garnish with sprigs of mint.

PAPAYA, BANANAS AND MANGOS

    1 papaya, peeled, seeded and sliced
    2 bananas, sliced
    1 mango, peeled and chopped
 ¼ cup orange juice
    1 T lemon juice
       coconut flakes or chopped nuts

Put fruit into a bowl. Combine orange juice and lemon juice, and pour it over the fruit. Serve in fruit cups garnished with coconut flakes or chopped nuts. Makes 2 or 3 servings.

CLASSIC FRUIT SALAD

    1 apple, chopped
    1 banana, sliced
 ½ cup pineapple chunks
 ½ cup raisins
 ½ cup chopped nuts
 ½ cup Coconut Cream*

In a bowl, combine fruit and nuts. Spoon salad into individual serving dishes and top fruit with 2 tablespoons of Coconut Cream. Makes 3 or 4 servings.

CRANBERRY RELISH

 ½ orange, including peel
 ½ cup cranberries
    2 T honey

Chop the orange. Put the cranberries, orange, and honey into a blender and blend until the fruit is coarsely chopped. Makes about ⅔ cup.

TROPICAL FRUIT BOWL

 ¼ cup shaved fresh coconut
    1 cup diced pineapple
    1 small papaya, peeled, seeded, and
          chopped
    1 orange, peeled and sectioned
    1 banana, sliced
 ½ lime, juice of
       watercress or salad greens
Garnish: coarsely ground nuts or Coconut Pie Shell* mix

Combine coconut and fruit in a salad bowl. Sprinkle the fruit with lime juice and toss lightly. Serve on a bed of watercress or salad greens. Makes 2 servings.

77

WHIPPED BANANAS

¼ t agar granules or 1 T flakes
¼ cup water
2 very ripe bananas, sliced
1 t lemon juice
2 T Honey
1 cup Coconut Cream*

Put agar granules and water into a saucepan and heat until granules are dissolved; set aside. Whirl bananas, lemon juice and honey in a blender until creamy. Add dissolved agar and coconut cream, blend until mixed. Pour into sherbet glasses and chill until firm. Makes 3 or 4 servings.

MANGOS IN GINGER SAUCE

2 mangos, peeled and chopped
2 T honey
1 slice ginger root, minced
1 T lemon juice
   shredded coconut

Put chopped mangos into a bowl. In a cup, combine honey, ginger and lemon juice; whip with a fork until creamy. Pour sauce over the mangos and mix until fruit is coated. Serve in individual dishes and top fruit with coconut. Makes 2 servings.

DRIED FRUIT COMPOTE

4 dried figs
4 dried prunes
½ cup dried apricots
2 T raisins
½ cup water
½ cup apple juice
   cinnamon stick, 1-inch long
1 T lemon juice
1 T honey

Put all ingredients into a small deep bowl and let stand 4 hours or overnight. Delicious for breakfast or lunch. Makes 2 servings.

PAPAYA AND BANANAS

1 papaya, peeled and seeded
2 bananas
2 T coconut flakes
2 T chopped nuts

Slice papaya and bananas. Arrange fruit on a salad plates and top with coconut and nuts. Makes 2 servings.

FRUIT SALAD

3 bananas, sliced
½ cup fresh or dried figs, chopped
½ cup dates, chopped
¼ cup chopped almonds
¼ cup chopped pecans
Garnish: shredded coconut

Combine bananas, dried fruit, and nuts. Makes 2 or 3 servings.

AUTUMN SALAD

1 large red apple, chopped
1 orange, seeded and chopped
1 cup pineapple chunks
  salad greens
  sprigs of mint

Combine fruit and serve over a bed of greens. Garnish with sprigs of mint. Makes 2 or 3 servings.

CALIFORNIA SALAD

1 orange
1 tangerine
1 grapefruit
1 avocado, chopped
1 t honey
1 T lemon juice
Garnish: grated coconut, fresh or dried

Peel, section and seed the citrus fruit. Cut fruit segments into bite-size pieces and put into a bowl with the chopped avocado. Mix the honey and lemon juice in a small bowl, and add any juice that has separated from the cut fruit. Pour the dressing over the salad and toss lightly. Makes 3 or 4 servings.

HAWAIIAN FRUIT SALAD

1 pineapple, peeled and cut in 1-inch cubes
1 papaya, cut in 1-inch cubes
2 bananas, sliced
½ cup fresh grated coconut or ½ cup dried flake coconut
¼ cup orange juice
Garnish: sprig of mint

Put the pineapple, papaya, bananas, and coconut into a salad bowl, pour orange juice over, and mix well. Makes 3 or 4 servings.

PAPAYA CREAM

2 papayas, peeled, seeded and chopped
1 slice fresh ginger root, minced
1 T lemon or lime juice
¾ cup Coconut Cream*
   coconut flakes

Put papaya, ginger and lemon juice into a blender and whip until smooth and creamy. Add coconut cream and blend about 5 seconds. Pour papaya cream into sherbet dishes and sprinkle with coconut flakes. Makes 3 or 4 servings.

FRUIT AMBROSIA

1 cup pineapple chunks
1 orange, chopped
1 banana, sliced
1 cup strawberries, sliced
¼ cup grated fresh coconut
2 T honey
2 T lemon
¼ cup orange juice

Put fruit into a bowl. Combine honey, lemon juice and orange juice. Mix well and pour over fruit. Makes 3 or 4 servings.

PEARS IN MINT SAUCE

2 pears, thinly sliced
3 T honey
1 t water
2 t lemon juice
3 drops oil of peppermint
½ cup blueberries

Put the pear slices into a bowl. In a cup, combine honey, water, lemon juice and oil of peppermint. Mix sauce thoroughly and pour over the pears. Chill for an hour. Serve garnished with blueberries. Makes 2 or 3 servings.

·BREADS & GRAINS·

SUN BREADS

The following two basic recipes are for making sun breads. They can also be used to make delicious crackers, noodles, dip-chips, tostada shells, and croutons. When making noodles, double the amount of tahini or nut butter. Nut butter and tahini make a softer, more absorbent product. Add your favorite herbs for variety. Caraway, dill, fines herbes, poppy seed, garlic, onion, or sweet basil are good additions for crackers. The dough can be rolled thin and cut into dip-chip sizes that can also be used as croutons to garnish salads or soups. Dry the dough shapes in the sun, in a dehydrator, or in a warm kitchen. If you are not going to use the dried product the same day, store it in the refrigerator in a sealed plastic bag, or freeze it.

MILLET SUN BREAD

¼ cup millet, ground into flour
½ cup whole-wheat flour
 1 T tahini
¼ cup water

Combine all ingredients and knead until smooth and elastic. Divide dough into two parts and roll each part into a thin sheet. Cut sheets into desired shapes. To make tostada shells, divide dough into 8 balls. Roll each ball into a very thin round, about 7 inches in diameter. Dry until crisp. Makes 8 shells.

WHOLE-WHEAT SUN BREAD

½ cup whole-wheat flour
2 t tahini, or 1 T Brazil nut butter
3 T water

Combine all ingredients and knead until smooth and elastic. Divide dough into two parts and roll each part into a thin sheet. Cut sheets into desired shapes. To make tostada shells, divide dough into 6 balls. Roll each ball into a 6-inch round. Dry until crisp. Makes 6 shells.

CORNMEAL TOSTADA SHELLS

½ cup cornmeal or corn flour
¼ cup whole-wheat flour
1 T tahini

Combine all ingredients and knead until smooth and elastic. Divide dough into 8 parts. On a floured surface, roll each ball into a 7-inch round. Dry until crisp. Makes 8 shells.

FOUR GRAIN CRACKERS

¼ cup oat flour
¼ cup rice flour
¼ cup millet flour
¼ cup wheat flour
⅓ cup water

Combine all ingredients and knead dough until smooth. Roll dough into a thin sheet and cut into desired shapes with a cookie cutter or knife. Dry until crisp. Makes about 5 dozen 2½-inch crackers.
VARIATION: Add ¼ cup ground nuts or seeds for a softer cracker.

BANANA BREAD

1 medium banana
1 cup whole-wheat flour
1 cup rolled oats, ground
1 T oil

Combine all ingredients and mix until well blended. Add a little more water if necessary. Dough should be stiff. Shape dough into a log. Refrigerate until ready to use. When ready to serve, cut bread into thin slices. Makes 1 small loaf.

GRANOLA

2 T honey
1 T oil
1 cup rolled oats
½ cup wheat germ
½ cup shredded coconut
¼ cup chopped almonds
¼ cup chopped pecans
2 T carob flour
  Almond Milk* or Coconut Milk*

Mix honey and oil until smooth. Put remaining ingredients into a large bowl, then dribble the honey mixture over the cereal. Stir until thoroughly mixed. Cover and refrigerate until ready to use. Serve plain or with Almond Milk or Coconut Milk. Makes about 2½ cups.

VARIATIONS: Serve with chopped bananas or berries. Use granola as a garnish for fresh fruits. Add raisins if desired. Use rolled, whole-wheat flakes instead of rolled oats.

WHOLE-WHEAT VEGETABLE CRACKERS

1 cup whole-wheat flour
2 t dried vegetable broth
⅓-½ cup water

Combine all ingredients and knead until smooth. Roll dough into a thin sheet and cut into desired shapes. Dry until crisp. Makes 3½ dozen 2½-inch crackers.

COCONUT-CAROB BREAD

½ cup carob flour
¼ cup shredded coconut
½ cup ground almonds
¼ cup water
2 T sesame seed

Combine all ingredients and make a very stiff dough. Roll dough into a log and wrap it in wax paper. Store log in the refrigerator until ready to use. Serve in very thin slices. Slices are delicious served with Honey Butter* or plain. Makes 1 small log.

SPROUTED GRAIN CHIPS

1 cup wheat, rye, or triticale sprouts
1 T tahini

Use a fine blade, grind sprouts. Add tahini to the ground sprouts and knead until well mixed. Dough will be sticky, so be sure your rolling surface is well floured. Divide dough into two parts and roll each into a thin sheet. Use a sharp knife to cut the sheet into chips or crackers. To make tostada shells, divide dough into 6 parts and roll each into a thin round. Makes 6 shells.

VARIATION: Use one part sprouted millet and two parts sprouted wheat. Grind millet and wheat sprouts.

PARSLEY NOODLES

    1   cup whole-wheat flour
    ¼   cup tahini
    ¼   cup water
    ¼   cup minced parsley
Sauce: Pesto*, Parsley Sauce*, or Sesame Tomato Sauce*

Combine all ingredients and knead until smooth and elastic. Divide dough into 3 parts. On a floured surface, roll out one part of the dough at a time into a very thin sheet. Cut sheets into strips that are about ¼-inch wide by 4 inches long. Drop each strip onto a cookie sheet to dry. Twisted and curled strips will make better noodles. When dried, the noodles will mound well on a plate, exposing more surface to absorb the accompanying sauce. Dry the noodles at room temperature or in a dehydrator until they are rigid. Serve noodles with Pesto, Parsley Sauce, or Sesame Tomato Sauce. Use about ¾ cup of sauce per serving. Makes 2 or 3 servings.

VARIATIONS: Use rye or triticale flour in place of whole-wheat. Use spinach or watercress instead of parsley.

GARLIC CROUTONS

    ¼   cup whole-wheat flour
    ½   cup rice flour
    1   T tahini
    1   T sunflower seed, ground
    ¼   clove garlic
    ¼   cup water

Combine all ingredients and knead until smooth. Roll dough into a thin sheet and cut into 1-inch by 1½-inch rectangles or diamonds. Dry until crisp. Use as dip-chips or as croutons in salads or as a garnish for soups. Makes 4 dozen chips.

PUMPKIN SEED WAFERS

    ¼   cup pumpkin seed, ground
    5   T water
    ½   cup rice flour
    ½   cup oat flour

Combine all ingredients and knead until smooth. Roll out dough into a thin sheet and cut into desired shapes. Dry until crisp. Makes about 2 dozen 2½-inch wafers.

·DESSERTS·

FRUIT CAKE

    6 dates, pitted
  ¼ cup raisins
    4 figs
  ¼ cup dried apples
  ¼ cup shredded coconut
  ¼ cup walnuts
  ¼ cup sunflower seed
    4 dried pear halves
    1 small banana
  ¼ t cinnamon
  ⅛ t allspice
  ⅛ t nutmeg
  ¼ cup whole-wheat flour
    1 cup oatmeal

Coarsely grind the first 8 ingredients and set aside. Mash banana and add spices; whip until smooth. Add flour to bananas, mix well, and then add oatmeal, and fruit mixture. Shape mixture into a loaf. Refrigerate until ready to use. Serve in very thin slices. Makes 1 loaf.

CRANBERRY WAFERS

  ¼ cup water
    1 cup ground oatmeal
    1 T ground, dried cranberries
    1 T honey
  ¼ cup whole-wheat flour

Mix all ingredients and knead until dough is smooth. Roll out into a thin sheet and cut into desired shapes with a cookie cutter. Dry until crisp. Makes 2 dozen wafers.

PUMPKIN CANDY

    1 cup pumpkin seed, ground
  ¼ cup grated fresh pumpkin
    2 T honey
       shredded coconut

Combine all ingredients and stir until well blended. Shape into 1-inch balls and roll in shredded coconut. Refrigerate until ready to serve. Makes about 18 balls.

RAISIN-NUT COOKIES

½ cup oatmeal, ground
¼ cup raisins, ground
2 T wheat germ
2 T almond butter
1 T honey

Combine all ingredients and knead until smooth. Roll dough into a 1-inch log. Wrap with plastic and chill. When ready to serve, cut into small slices. The dough may be rolled into a thin sheet and cut with a cookie cutter. The rolled cookies can be served moist or dried. Makes about 2 dozen small cookies.

CASHEW CONFECTIONS

2 T honey
1 cup cashews, finely ground

Combine honey and ground cashews; knead with your hands until well mixed. Add a little more honey if mixture is too crumbly. Form the confection into balls or flatten mixture into a ½-inch-thick sheet. Cut into squares. Makes about 1 dozen confections. VARIATIONS: Add shredded coconut, currants, chopped walnuts, or carob flour. Use confection to fill dates or dried apricots. Ground almonds or other ground nuts or seeds may be used in place of cashews.

STRAWBERRY PIE

¼ cup water
1 t agar granules or 2 T agar flakes
¼ cup honey
1½ cups orange juice
3 bananas, sliced
1 pie crust, Coconut* or Nut*
1½ cups strawberries, sliced

Heat the water and agar until granules are dissolved. Cool to lukewarm and add the honey. Stir until honey dissolves and add orange juice. Pour mixture into a blender and whip until smooth. Put a layer of sliced bananas over the bottom of the pie shell and top with the strawberries. Pour over the orange mixture and refrigerate until set. Serves 6 to 8.

BRAZIL NUT COOKIES

½ cup whole grain flour
12 Brazil nuts, ground
1 T honey
2 T water
⅛ t vanilla

In a mixing bowl, combine flour and ground nuts. In a cup, mix the honey, water, and vanilla. When honey is dissolved, pour over flour mixture. Mix dough until smooth. Roll dough into a ¼-inch sheet and cut with cookie cutters into desired shapes. Dry or serve moist. Makes 2 dozen small cookies.

PERSIMMON-CRANBERRY JELL

¼ cup water
½ t granular agar or 1 T agar flakes
2 ripe persimmons, seeded and chopped
¼ cup cranberries
3 T honey
1 T lemon juice
   dash cinnamon

Put the water and agar into a saucepan and heat until agar has dissolved completely. Cool to lukewarm. Pour the agar water and the remaining ingredients into a blender and whip until creamy. Pour mixture into sherbet dishes and refrigerate to jell. Makes 2 servings.

NUT PIE SHELL

¾ cup ground almonds
1 T oil
1 T honey
¼ cup oatmeal, ground

Put all the ingredients into a blender and blend until thoroughly mixed. If the dough will not stick together, add a little more honey. Roll dough out between two sheets of wax paper. Remove top piece of wax paper and turn pastry side down into a pie plate. Remove the second piece of wax paper. Makes 1 shell.

CASHEW ICE CREAM

1 t agar granules or 2 T agar flakes
2½ cups water
¾ cup cashew nut butter
¼ cup honey
1 t vanilla
1 T lemon juice

Put the agar and water in a saucepan and heat until agar granules are dissolved. Agar flakes may require simmering several minutes before they are ready; follow the directions on the jar. When agar water is ready, remove from the heat and cool to lukewarm. Put agar water and remaining ingredients into a blender and whip for one minute. Pour the mixture into an ice cream freezer. Following the freezer instructions, freeze until firm. Store ice cream in the refrigerator freezer until ready to serve. Makes about 1 quart.

VARIATIONS: Omit one cup of water and add one cup of fruit pulp just before pouring into the freezer. Bananas, strawberries, or peaches make excellent fruit-flavored ice creams. For carob ice cream, add ¼ cup carob flour. Add ½ cup chopped walnuts or pecans for a delicious flavor and a crunchy texture. Substitute any kind of nut or seed butter for cashew butter.

DATE-NUT ICE CREAM

    2 cups water
    1 t agar granules or 2 T agar flakes
    1 cup chopped dates
    2 T honey
    ¾ cup ground cashews or almonds
    ½ cup chopped nuts

Put the water and agar into a saucepan and heat until agar is dissolved. Cool to luke-warm. Put warm agar water and dates into a blender and blend until smooth. Add honey and ground cashews; blend until creamy. Add chopped walnuts and pour mixture into an ice cream freezer. Freeze until firm according to freezer instructions, then store in the refrigerator freezer until ready to use. Makes about 1 quart.

SUNFLOWER SEED ROLL

    1 cup cashews, ground
    1 cup sunflower seed
    1 T honey
       dash of vanilla

Put all ingredients into a bowl and mix thoroughly. Roll candy into a 1-inch roll. Wrap in wax paper and chill. When ready to serve, slice candy into ½-inch circles. Makes about 1½ dozen pieces.

PERSIMMON CREAM PIE

    ¼ cup water
    1 t granular agar or 2 T agar flakes
    4 very ripe persimmons, seeded and chopped
    ¼ cup honey
    ¼ cup finely ground coconut
    ¼ t cinnamon
    1 Coconut Pie Shell*
       shredded coconut

Put the water and agar into a saucepan and heat until agar has dissolved. Cool to luke-warm. Put the persimmons, honey, coconut and cinnamon into a blender and blend until smooth. Add agar mixture and blend fifteen seconds. Pour pie filling into a Coconut Pie Shell and decorate with a little shredded coconut. Refrigerate to jell. Serves 6.

HAZEL NUT THINS

    ¼ cup hazel nuts, ground
    2 T water
    ½ cup rice flour
    1 T honey

Mix all ingredients and knead until the dough is smooth. Roll dough into a thin sheet (1/16-inch to 1/8-inch thick). Cut with a cookie cutter. Dry until crisp. Makes about 2 dozen small cookies.

OATMEAL COOKIES

½ cup honey
½ small banana
½ t vanilla
1 t cinnamon
1 cup rolled oats
½ cup whole-wheat flour
½ cup pecans, chopped
¼ cup almonds, chopped
½ cup raisins

Combine honey, banana, vanilla, and cinnamon, whip until creamy, and add remaining ingredients. Mix well and shape into flat cookies. Makes 2 dozen.

VARIATIONS: Add ½ cup shredded coconut. Use carob flour instead of whole-wheat.

SESAME TAFFY

1 cup sesame seed, ground
2 T sesame oil
2 T honey
  dash vanilla
  dash almond extract

Blend all ingredients until thoroughly mixed. Press taffy out on a platter into a ⅓-inch thick sheet. Cut in squares and chill until ready to serve. Makes about 1½ dozen squares.

APPLE SHERBET

2 apples, cored and chopped
2 oranges, peeled and seeded
½ lemon, juice of
¼ cup honey
1 large, ripe banana, sliced

Put all ingredients into a blender and blend until smooth. Pour fruit mixture into a one-quart ice cream freezer and freeze according to the freezer instructions. When sherbet is frozen, store in the refrigerator freezer until ready to serve. Sherbet can also be made by pouring the mixture into ice cube trays and freezing. When frozen, turn on the blender and add the frozen cubes one by one. Blend until creamy and serve at once in chilled sherbet glasses. Makes about 1 quart.

PEACH CONFECTIONS

3 oz dried peaches, ground
2 T almond butter
4 Brazil nuts, ground
1 T honey

Mix all ingredients until smooth. Shape mixture into small balls or patties. Refrigerate until ready to serve. Makes 12 patties.

BANANA CREAM

2 ripe bananas, sliced
   water

Put the banana slices into a plastic bag and freeze in the refrigerator freezer. (Bananas can be frozen whole and then cut into slices.) Turn on blender and add the frozen banana slices one at a time until a thick banana cream is formed. Add a little water if necessary. Serve at once in chilled sherbet glasses. Makes 2 or 3 servings.
VARIATIONS: Add ¼ cup of fruit juice or ¼ cup fresh fruit pulp. Add six walnut or pecan halves and blend five seconds. Add two teaspoons of honey dissolved in two tablespoons of water. Garnish with a small piece of fruit or chopped nuts.

ICE BOX COOKIES

½ cup oatmeal, ground
¼ cup pecans, ground
4 Brazil nuts, ground
2 T almond butter
1 T honey
⅛ t cinnamon
   pinch allspice

Combine all ingredients and knead until smooth. Roll dough into a 1-inch log and wrap with plastic. Refrigerate until needed. Before serving, cut log into ½-inch slices. Makes 2 dozen slices.

90

APPLE PIE

1 T lemon juice
¼ cup honey
¼ t nutmeg
½ t cinnamon
3 cups finely chopped apples
¼ cup raisins
¼ cup ground cashews
1 pie shell

Put the lemon juice, honey, nutmeg, and cinnamon into a small bowl and whip until creamy. Put the apples, raisins, and ground cashews into a large bowl and mix. Dribble the honey mixture over the apples and stir until fruit is well coated. Spoon the filling into a pie shell and refrigerate until ready to serve. Pie is most tasty if served soon after making. Makes 6 servings.

BLUEBERRY PIE

3 cups blueberries
½ cup chopped dates
½ cup raisins
½ cup walnuts
2 bananas, sliced
   cinnamon

Put blueberries, dates, raisins and walnuts into a blender and mix until creamy. Line a pie plate with sliced bananas and cover with the blueberry mixture. Sprinkle with cinnamon and chill until pie jells. Makes 6 to 8 servings.

PAPAYA PIE

1 t agar granules or 2 T agar flakes
½ cup water
3 T honey
1 cup orange juice
1 T lemon juice
1 Nut Pie Shell*
2 cups sliced papaya
   Coconut Cream*

Heat the agar and water in a saucepan until dissolved, cool until lukewarm, and pour into a blender. Add honey, orange juice, and lemon juice. Blend until smooth. Fill the pie shell with papaya slices and pour orange juice mixture evenly over the fruit. Refrigerate to jell. Serve plain or with a dollop of Coconut Cream. Makes 6 to 8 servings.

COCONUT PIE SHELL

1 cup shredded coconut
¼ cup oatmeal
1 T honey
3 T whole-wheat flour
1 T water

Combine all ingredients in a blender and blend until dough is granular. Roll dough out between two sheets of wax paper. Remove top piece of wax paper and turn pastry side down into a pie plate. Remove the second piece of wax paper. Makes 1 shell.

VARIATION: Instead of rolling out the dough, crumble it over fruit or Coconut Cream*, Banana Cream*, or Cashew Ice Cream*.

COCONUT MACAROONS

¼ cup tahini
2 T honey
3 T water
¼ t vanilla
2 cups dried coconut flakes
¼ cup shredded coconut

Put the tahini, honey, water, and vanilla into a blender. Blend until mixture is creamy. Put the coconut flakes into a bowl and pour the tahini mixture over it. Mix until flakes are well coated. Form mixture into walnut-sized balls, roll in shredded coconut, and refrigerate. Makes 1½ dozen balls.

VARIATIONS: Add ¼ cup raisins and/or chopped nuts.

·BEVERAGES·

APPLE-PEAR NECTAR

1 apple, chopped
1 pear, chopped
1 t lemon juice
1 cup water or juice

Put all ingredients into a blender and liquefy. Makes 2 or 3 servings.

PRUNE SHAKE

6 prunes, pitted
½ cup water
1 frozen banana

Soak the prunes in the water until plump. Liquefy the prunes in the soaking water. Cut the banana into 1-inch pieces and add to prune mixture while blending. Makes 1 large thick shake that can be eaten with a spoon.

DRIED FRUIT MILK

½ cup dried fruit: dates, prunes, or apricots
2 cups warm water

Soak fruit in water until plumped. Pour fruit and water into a blender and blend until smooth. Makes 2 servings.

COCONUT MILK

1 cup shredded dry coconut, ground to butter
2 cups water
honey to taste

Put all ingredients in a blender and whip until smooth and creamy. Coconut milk is delicious as a beverage or served over cereal. Makes about 3 cups.

CARROT-APPLE DRINK

2 cups carrot juice
1 cup apple juice
2 t honey
    dash of cloves

Combine all ingredients in a blender and mix until smooth. Makes 4 servings.

LIME OR LEMONADE

2 cups water
1 lemon or lime, juice of
2 t honey, more or less to taste

Combine water, citrus juice and honey in a blender and mix well. Serve iced with a sprig of fresh mint. Makes 2 glasses.

WINTER APRICOT DRINK

½ lb dried apricots
¼ cup honey
 4 cups water

Soak apricots in honey-water overnight. Pour plumped apricots and soaking water into a blender and blend until smooth. Makes 4 servings.

ALMOND MILK

1 cup almonds, ground to butter
3 cups water

Combine almonds and water in a blender and blend 1 minute. Strain milk through cheesecloth and serve chilled. Nut residue may be used in cookies. Makes 4 servings. VARIATIONS: Sweeten to taste with honey. Add a dash of vanilla, and a dash of nutmeg or cinnamon.

CASHEW MILK

1 cup cashews, finely ground
4 cups water
    honey

Put ground cashews and water into a blender and blend for one minute. Serve plain or sweeten with a little honey. Makes a little more than 1 quart.

ORANGE-BANANA DRINK

3 cups orange juice
3 ripe bananas, sliced

Blend orange juice and banana slices until smooth. Makes 4 servings.

V-3 JUICE

3 cups carrot juice
¼ cup spinach juice
½ cup celery juice
4 sprigs parsley

Combine the three juices. Pour into 4 glasses and top each with a sprig of parsley. Makes 4 servings.

V-4 JUICE

1 cup carrot juice
½ cup celery juice
¼ cup parsley juice
¼ cup spinach juice
2 sprigs parsley

Combine the juices and pour into 2 glasses.

Top each with a sprig of parsley. Makes 2 servings.

V-5 JUICE

1¼ cups carrot juice
¼ cup string bean juice
½ cup cucumber juice
½ cup celery juice
½ cup lettuce juice
3 sprigs celery leaves

Combine the juices. Serve in glasses topped with sprigs of celery leaves. Makes 3 glasses.

V-6 VERDE JUICE

1 cup celery juice
½ cup cucumber juice
½ cup cabbage juice
½ cup green pepper juice
¼ cup parsley juice
¼ cup spinach juice

Mix all juices. This is a refreshing, thirst-quenching beverage. Makes 3 cups.

APPLE-CRAN JUICE

2¾ cups apple juice
¼ cup cranberry juice

Combine juices. This lovely pink juice is as delicious as it looks. Makes 2 cups.

ORANGE JUICE COCKTAIL

2 cups orange juice
1 banana, sliced
4 dates, pitted
2 T wheat germ

Blend all ingredients until smooth. Makes 3 servings.

METRIC MEASUREMENTS

U.S.	Metric
1 quart (32 fl. oz.)	. . 9.5 decilitres
1 pint (16 fl. oz.)	. 4.7 decilitres
1 cup (8 fl. oz.)	. 2.4 decilitres
1 tablespoon (1/3 fl. oz.)	1.5 centilitres
1 teaspoon (1/9 fl. oz.)	.5 centilitres
1 pound (16 oz.)	approximately 500 grams
1/2 pound (8 oz.)	approximately 250 grams
1/4 pound (4 oz.)	approximately 120 grams
(1 oz.)	approximately 30 grams

BIBLIOGRAPHY

THE FIRST PRIMATES

Campbell, B. G. *Humankind Emerging.* Boston: Little, Brown, 1976.

Goodall, J. *In the Shadow of Man.* Boston: Houghton Mifflin, 1971.

Hulse, F. S. *The Human Species.* New York: Random House, 1971.

Pilbeam, D. *The Ascent of Man.* New York: Macmillan, 1972.

Pilbeam, D. "Newly Recognized Mandible of *Ramapithecus.*" *Nature* 222 (1969), 1093.

Schaller, G. B. *The Year of the Gorilla.* Chicago: University of Chicago Press, 1964.

Simons, E. L. "On the Mandible of *Ramapithecus.*" *Proceedings of the National Academy of Sciences* 51 (1964), 528.

Simons, E. L. "The Earliest Apes." *Scientific American* 217 (1967), 28-35.

Simons, E. L. *Primate Evolution.* New York: Macmillan, 1972.

Stein, P. L., and Rowe, B. M. *Physical Anthropology.* New York: McGraw-Hill, 1974.

Van Valen, L., and Sloan, R. E. "The Earliest Primates." *Science* 150, no. *3697* (1965), 743-45.

AUSTRALOPITHECINES

Crompton, A., and Hiiemae, K. "How Mammalian Molar Teeth Work." *Discovery* 5 (1969), 23.

Day, M., and Napier, J. R. "Hominid Fossils from Bed I, Olduvai Gorge, Tanganyika: Fossil Foot Bones." *Nature* 201 (1964), 968.

Jolly, C. J. "The Seed Eaters: a new model of hominid differentiation based on a baboon analogy." *Man* 5 (1970), 5.

Krantz, G. "Brain Size and Hunting Ability in Earliest Man." *Current Anthropology* 9 (1966), 5.

Lee, R., and De Vore, I. *Man the Hunter.* Chicago: Aldine, 1968.

Lieberman, P., and Crelin, E. "Phonetic Ability and Related Anatomy of the New Born and Adult Human, Neandertal Man, and the Chimpanzee." *American Anthropologist* 74 (1972), 3.

Napier, J. R. "Fossil Hand Bones from Olduvai Gorge." *Nature* 196 (1962), 409.

Pilbeam, D. *The Ascent of Man.* New York: Macmillan, 1972.

Robinson, J. "The Genera and Species of *Australopithecus.*" *American Journal of Physical Anthropology* 12 (1954), 181.

Tobias, P. *Olduvai Gorge,* vol. 2. Cambridge, England: Cambridge University Press, 1967.

HOMO ERECTUS

Caillas, A. "Pollen: Its Harvest — Its Properties and Uses." *The Golden Pollen.* Edited by M. McCormick. Yakima, Wash.: Yakima Printing, 1960.

Clark, W. E. L. *The Fossil Evidence for Human Evolution.* Chicago: University of Chicago Press, 1964.

Coon, C. *The Origin of Races.* New York: Knopf, 1962.

DeLumley, H. "A Paleolithic Camp in Nice." *Scientific American* 220 (1969), 5.

Howells, W. *Mankind in the Making: The Story of Human Evolution.* New York: Doubleday, 1959.

Leach, E. *A Runaway World?* London: British Broadcasting Co., 1967.

Stone, I. "Studies of a Mammalian Enzyme System for Producing Evolutionary Evidence on Man." *American Journal of Physical Anthropology* 23 (1965), 83-86.

Von Koenigswald, G. H. R. *Meeting Prehistoric Man.* New York: Harper, 1956.

HOMO SAPIENS

Borde, F. *The Old Stone Age.* New York: McGraw-Hill, 1968.

Brace, C. L. "Cultural Factors in the Evolution of the Human Dentition." *Culture and the Evolution of Man.* Edited by M. F. A. Montague. New York: Oxford University Press, 1962.

Brace, C. L. "Refocusing on the Neandertal Problem." *American Anthropologist* 64, no. 4 (1962), 730-32.

Clark, W. E. L. *The Fossil Evidence for Human Evolution.* Chicago: University of Chicago Press, 1964.

Constable, G. *Emergence of Man: The Neandertals.* New York: Time-Life Books, 1973.

Lee, R. "What Hunters do for a Living, or, How to make out on scarce resources." *Man the Hunter.* Edited by R. Lee and I. De Vore. Chicago: Aldine, 1968.

"Toxicants Occurring Naturally in Foods." Washington, D.C.: National Academy of Sciences, 1973.

Simons, E. L. *Primate Evolution: An Introduction to Man's Place in Nature.* New York: Macmillan, 1972.

Solecki, R. S. *Shanidar: The First Flower People.* New York: Knopf, 1971.

Stein, P. L., and Rowe, B. M. *Physical Anthropology.* New York: McGraw-Hill, 1974.

Straus, W., and Cave, A. "Pathology and the Posture of Neandertal Man." *The Quarterly Review of Biology* 32 (1957), 348-63.

AGRICULTURE

Edlin, H. L. *Plants and Man.* New York: Natural History Press, 1969.

Jennings, J. *Prehistory of North America.* New York: McGraw-Hill, 1968.

Kirschmann, J. D. *Nutrition Almanac.* New York: McGraw-Hill, 1975.

Leonard, J. N. *The First Farmers.* New York: Little, Brown, 1973.

MacNeish, R. "Ancient Mesoamerican Civilization." *Science* 145, no. 3606 (1964), 531-538.

MacNeish, R. "Preliminary Archaeological Investigations in the Sierra de Tamaulipas, Mexico." *American Philosophical Society Transactions* 48 (1958), 6.

MacNeish, R. Second Annual Report, Ayacucho Archaeological-Botanical Project. Cambridge, Mass.: Robert S. Peabody Foundation, 1970.

Mangelsdorf, P., MacNeish, R., and Galinat, W. "Domestication of Corn." *Science* 143, no. 3606 (1964), 538-544.

Willey, G. *An Introduction to American Archaeology: North and Middle America.* Englewood Cliffs, N.J.: Prentice-Hall, 1966.

THE ORIGINAL DIET

Airola, P. *Are You Confused?* Phoenix: Health Plus, 1971.

Davis, A. *Let's Get Well.* New York: Harcourt Brace Jovanovich, 1965.

"Milk and Milk Products in Human Nutrition." Rome: Food and Agriculture Organization of the United Nations, 1972.

Hunter, B. T. *Fermented Foods and Beverages: An Old Tradition.* New Canaan, Conn. Keats, 1973.

Jacobson, M. F. *Eater's Digest: The Consumer's Fact Book of Food Additives and Are They Safe?* New York: Doubleday, 1972.

Lapp, F. M. *Diet for a Small Planet.* New York: Ballantine, 1971.

Marx, H. L., Jr. *The World Food Crisis.* New York: H. W. Wilson, 1975.

Recommended Dietary Allowances. Washington, D.C.: National Academy of Sciences, 1974.

Toxicants Occurring Naturally in Foods. Washington, D.C.: National Academy of Sciences, 1973.

Rodale, J. I. "Milk, the Imperfect Food." *Prevention 27* (1975), 11:169.

Rosenberg. H., with Feldzamen, A. N. *The Book of Vitamin Therapy.* New York: Berkeley.

Requirements of Ascorbic Acid, Vitamin D, Vitamin B-12, Folate, and Iron. Technical Report Series, no. 452. Geneva: World Health Organization, 1970.

Whyte, K. C. *The Complete Yogurt Cookbook.* San Francisco: Troubador, 1970.

FASTING

Airola, P. *Are You Confused?* Phoenix: Health Plus, 1971.

Berman, S. "Fasting: An old cure for fat, a new treatment for schizophrenia." *Science Digest* 1 (1976), 27-31.

Burton, B. T. *Human Nutrition.* New York: McGraw-Hill, 1976.

Cott, A. *Fasting: The Ultimate Diet.* New York: Bantam, 1975.

Shelton, H. M. *Fasting Can Save Your Life.* Chicago: Natural Hygiene, 1967.

Young, V. R., and Schrimshaw, N. S. "The Physiology of Starvation." *Scientific American* 225, no. 4 (1971), 14-21.

SODIUM

Airola, P. *Are You Confused?* Phoenix: Health Plus, 1971.

Bieler, H. G. *Food Is Your Best Medicine.* New York: Random House, 1968.

Recommended Dietary Allowances. Washington, D.C.: National Academy of Sciences, 1974.

Kirschmann, J. D. *Nutrition Almanac.* New York: McGraw-Hill, 1975.

Rodale, J. I. *The Complete Book of Minerals for Health.* Emmaus, Pa.: Rodale Press, 1975.

OIL

Clark, L. *Know Your Nutrition.* New Canaan, Conn.: Keats, 1973.

Pyke, M. *Food Science and Technology.* London: Murray, 1968.

Vegetable Oil: The Unsaturated Facts. Charlestown, Mass.: Talking Food, 1971.

FRUITS AND VEGETABLES

Carcione, J. *The Greengrocer — The Consumers Guide to Fruits and Vegetables.* San Francisco: Chronicle Books, 1972.

Kadans, J. M. *Encyclopedia of Fruits, Vegetables, Nuts and Seeds for Healthful Living.* New York: Parker, 1973.

Moyer, W. C. *The Buying Guide for Fresh Fruits, Vegetables, Herbs and Nuts.* Fullerton, Ca.: Blue Goose, 1976.

Whyte, K. C. *The Complete Sprouting Cookbook.* San Francisco: Troubador Press, 1973.

DEHYDRATION OF PRODUCE

Anderson, M. L., and Andrews, J. M. *Drying Food Nature's Way.* Salem, Ore.: Panther, 1974.

Densley, B. *The ABC's of Home Food Dehydration.* Bountiful, Utah: Horizon, 1975.

How to Dry Fruits and Vegetables at Home. New York: Doubleday, 1975.

Hobson, P. *Home Drying Vegetables, Fruits and Herbs.* Charlotte, Vt.: Garden Way, 1974.

Johnson, G. *A Guide to Preserving Foods in Your Food Dehydrator.* Riverside, Ca.: Kountry Kitchen, 1975.

Wheeler, E. *Home Food Dehydration: The Hows, What, and Why.* Seattle, Wash.: Craftsman and Met, 1974.

HERB TEAS

Adrian, A. and Dennis. *Herbal Tea Book.* San Francisco: Health, 1967.

Hutchens, A. R. *Indian Herbology of North America.* Ontario, Canada: Merco, 1974.

Kloss, J. *Back to Eden.* Coalmont, Tenn.: Longview, 1939.

Lust, J. *The Herb Book.* New York: Bantam, 1974.

Meyer, J. *The Herbalist.* New York: Rand McNally, 1960.

Rose, J. *Herbs & Things.* New York: Grosset & Dunlap, 1976.

INDEX

106

NOTES: